AF589271

Persiana
ONE

Persiana
ONE

ONE PAN. ONE TRAY. ONE POT.

SABRINA GHAYOUR

MITCHELL
BEAZLEY

For those who love food as much as I do and who take joy from feeding others, this one is for you... I hope this book helps to make your life a little easier.

MITCHELL BEAZLEY

First published in Great Britain in 2026
by Mitchell Beazley, an imprint of
Octopus Publishing Group Ltd
Carmelite House
50 Victoria Embankment
London EC4Y 0DZ
www.octopusbooks.co.uk

An Hachette UK Company
www.hachette.co.uk

The authorized representative in the EEA
is Hachette Ireland, 8 Castlecourt Centre,
Dublin 15, D15 XTP3, Ireland
(email: info@hbgi.ie)

Distributed in the US by Hachette Book Group,
1290 Avenue of the Americas, 4th and 5th Floors,
New York, NY 10104

Distributed in Canada by Canadian Manda
Group, 664 Annette St., Toronto,
Ontario, Canada M6S 2C8

ISBN: 978 1 78325 610 5
eISBN: 978 1 78325 611 2

A CIP catalogue record for this book
is available from the British Library.

Printed and bound in China.

10 9 8 7 6 5 4 3 2 1

Publisher: Kate Fox
Senior Managing Editor: Sybella Stephens
Copy Editor: Jo Richardson
Art Director: Jaz Bahra
Photographer: Kris Kirkham
Food Stylist: Laura Field
Props Stylist: Agathe Gits
Senior Production Manager: Peter Hunt

Contents

Introduction

Sometimes I look around my kitchen when I'm cooking and it seems like a tornado has quietly ripped through it behind my back without me knowing! The older I get, the more I prefer less mess in the kitchen and more simplicity in recipe ingredients and methods. This book is based on the idea that you can cook some fantastic meals using just one tray, one pan, one pot or one bowl, or assemble a meal into one dish, and STILL produce the most fantastically flavourful results.

The idea is simple enough, but I haven't been too literal about it. I've still recommended pairings with other dishes that will make it a bigger meal or more of a feast, and you might have to mix something in a bowl before you pour it into a tray for cooking. What's more important to me is that you have faith in the fact that I have done all the thinking for you – I've scaled back on ingredients where I can, simplified methods and process as much as possible and I've been mindful to create the minimum amount of waste and washing up, too. It's a win on so many levels.

Over the last 12 years since my first book, I've learned a lot about where my culinary strengths lie and have combined them with your feedback. There are a few principles I've always stuck to when creating new recipes, and although some dishes have been simplified and tweaked to make them easier and more accessible, my three key values still hold true: my recipes must be simple, flavourful and, as far as possible, economical.

There are no good cooks or bad cooks, only cooks who have time, confidence and perhaps a little experience under their belts. All these things can be achieved when you find recipes that work for you by making your life a bit easier. As ever with my food, I wholeheartedly encourage you to chop and change ingredients to suit your mood, budget, preference or to use up whatever you have at home. If you can't find an ingredient, just leave it out! Not everything needs a replacement. Cooking this way will help you gain confidence which in turn will encourage you to cook more often. We all crave simple recipes that involve minimal effort and kitchen equipment and less washing up, but still deliver big on flavour, and that's exactly what this book is all about.

There is something in this book to suit everyone and every occasion, whether it's a quick snack for just you or a special occasion meal for a crowd, so fret not – do what I do and have a read, get your mini post-its out, then get cooking!

Sabrina Ghayour

Really Useful Staples

In this chapter, you'll find lots of great base recipes that can be easily tweaked in different ways to help make your meals easier and more flavourful. From multi-purpose spice blends and flavoured butters to deliciously simple rice, pasta ideas and easy chicken dinners... a one-stop shop for flavour inspiration that will be indispensable in your kitchen.

Three Ways with… Spice Blends

Having long relied on traditional shop-bought spice blends such as baharat and ras el hanout, over the years I have developed my own spice blends for use at home, which I gave names to only relatively recently. These really have proven to be incredibly useful and versatile for me, so it's high time I shared them with you and gave you plenty of ideas for how to use them. And yes, that does mean I suggest you double the quantities, but start with a single batch and get to know your way around each one first.

Bazaar Spice Blend

A wonderfully easy blend to use in a wide varieties of ways, from simply coating meats and fish for roasting or pan-frying to using in rice, potato and grain dishes as well as marinades, salads and dressings. It also adds incredible flavour and aroma to dips like hummus and also makes the perfect blend for the simplest of flatbread recipes (see below).

2 teaspoons dried oregano
2 teaspoons paprika
1 heaped teaspoon garlic granules
1 teaspoon ground ginger
1 teaspoon sumac

HOW TO USE

For pan-frying white meat, fish, seafood, halloumi cheese and green vegetables: Simply drizzle a little oil and sprinkle a generous amount of the Bazaar Spice Blend over whatever you are cooking and pan-fry, seasoning with Maldon sea salt flakes to bring out the flavour. A great tip for roasting salmon fillets is to preheat the oven to 220°C, 200°C fan (425°F), Gas Mark 7, sprinkle a generous amount of Bazaar Spice Blend all over the exposed flesh of the salmon (without any oil) and roast on a baking paper-lined baking tray for just 11 minutes for the perfect result. You will never cook your salmon any other way again!

For super-quick flatbreads without any yeast, resting or rising: Mix together 200g (7oz) of Greek-style yogurt, 200g (7oz) of self-raising flour, 1 teaspoon of baking powder, 1 tablespoon of Bazaar Spice Blend, 2 tablespoons of olive oil and a generous amount of Maldon sea salt flakes. Bring the ingredients together with your hands to form a dough, turn out on to your work surface dusted with a little extra flour and knead for 1 minute. Roughly divide the dough into4 portions, roll into balls and flatten between your palms, or using a rolling pin if preferred, until 5mm (¼ inch) thick. Heat a heavy-based dry frying pan over a medium-high heat, add one flatbread at a time and cook for about 2 minutes on each side. Don't be tempted to flatten the breads in the pan, as you want to encourage a natural rise and some nice browning. Transfer the cooked flatbreads to a plate while you cook the rest, or refrigerate half the dough and use within 24 hours. Great for serving with dips, stews, koftas and curries.

Persiana Spice Blend

This blend is featured on the cover of my debut cookbook *Persiana*, released in 2014, which I originally created for one of my signature dishes in that book – a slow-roasted spice-perfumed lamb. This highly fragrant blend is ideal for roasted meats, grills, root vegetables and squashes but also great with game, poultry, oily fish and seafood.

2 teaspoons ground cumin

2 handfuls of dried edible rose petals, finely ground in a spice or coffee grinder (optional)

2 teaspoons ground coriander

1 teaspoon garlic granules

1 teaspoon sumac

1 teaspoon ground cinnamon

1 teaspoon dried lime powder, or dried limes finely ground in a spice or coffee grinder

¼ teaspoon cayenne pepper

HOW TO USE

For soups, stews and pie fillings: Simply add a generous amount of the Persiana Spice Blend when softening your onions and cook for a couple of minutes, then follow with your chosen ingredients. It's such a wonderfully aromatic way to give favourite recipes an interesting twist.

For a spiced butter to add when frying or roasting white meat, seafood, game and vegetables: Leave a 250g (9oz) block of salted butter out of the refrigerator until it reaches room temperature. Put into a mixing bowl, add 2 tablespoons of the Persiana Spice Blend and mix together really well. You can add the finely grated zest of 1 unwaxed orange, lime or lemon to give the spiced butter a zesty citrus finish. Decant the spiced butter on to a piece of baking paper and roughly form into a sausage shape (it will form a perfect shape once you have wrapped it up), then roll it up in the paper and twist the ends as tightly as you can (like a sweet wrapper) so that you have a solid log of butter. Refrigerate for 4 hours or overnight until firm, then slice into portions.

Stuff the spiced butter under the skin of a chicken before roasting, or add it for the final 10 minutes of roasting meats or vegetables. When pan-frying meat, chicken or fish, once one side is cooked and you have turned the ingredient over to cook the other side, add the spiced butter, continue cooking and then baste with the butter before serving.

You can freeze any remaining portions and use them in cooking from frozen.

Flavour Spice Blend

This earthy blend of spices is especially good for roasted meats, root vegetables and squashes, and is also the perfect combination for kebabs such as shawarmas or koftas. Even more versatile than that, it can be added to soups, stews, tagines, pies and even shepherd's pie for maximum flavour and to inject a little Middle Eastern magic.

1 teaspoon ground cinnamon
1 teaspoon ground cumin
1 teaspoon ground turmeric
1 teaspoon ground coriander
1 teaspoon paprika
1 teaspoon garlic granules
¼ teaspoon cracked black pepper

HOW TO USE

For soups, stews and pie fillings: Simply add a generous amount of the Flavour Spice Blend when softening your onions and cook for a couple of minutes, then follow with your chosen ingredients.

For kebabs or shawarma: Using either boneless, skinless chicken thighs or lamb leg steaks, simply mix together some of the Flavour Spice Blend (about 2 tablespoons per 500g/1lb 2oz meat) with a little natural yogurt, a drizzle of olive oil, 1–2 crushed garlic cloves, a good squeeze of lemon juice and Maldon sea salt flakes to season in a large bowl. Add the chicken or lamb and then, using your hands, mix well to coat in the marinade. Leave to marinate at room temperature for 30 minutes (refrigerate if marinating for longer).

To cook the marinated chicken, preheat the oven to 220°C, 200°C fan (425°F), Gas Mark 7. Lay the chicken thighs on a baking tray lined with baking paper and bake for 35–40 minutes until cooked through. Remove from the oven and shred the meat using a good knife, then serve in wraps or pittas with natural yogurt, chilli sauce, tomatoes and onion.

To cook the marinated lamb leg steaks, heat a frying pan over a high heat, drizzle in a little oil and pan-fry the steaks for 4–5 minutes on each side (or more if desired). Remove from the pan to a warmed plate, cover with foil and leave to rest for a few minutes, then slice thinly and serve as above.

Three Ways with... Butter Bombs

I've always said that butter makes everything better. I find keeping some flavoured butter portions in the fridge or freezer can prove very handy when you need to transform a humble ingredient into something more special. Here are three wonderful butter blends, perfect for almost every occasion.

The Garlicky One

VEGETARIAN

This is perfect with fish, seafood, poultry, red meat and even potatoes, paneer and halloumi cheese or tofu. You can add it to a pan on the hob or a baking tray in the oven a few minutes before you finish cooking your ingredients. It's also great mixed into some cooked pasta, or stirred through leftover cooked grains such as rice.

- 250g (9oz) salted butter, at room temperature
- 3 large garlic cloves, minced or crushed
- ½ small packet (about 15g/½oz) of flat leaf parsley, finely chopped
- ½ small packet (about 15g/½oz) of fresh coriander, finely chopped
- ½ small packet (about 15g/½oz) of dill, finely chopped
- ½ small packet (about 10g/¼oz) of chives, very thinly sliced
- 1 teaspoon cumin seeds
- 1 teaspoon coriander seeds
- generous amount of freshly ground black pepper

Put all the ingredients in a mixing bowl and stir together. Use a spatula to decant the mixture on to a piece of baking paper.

Wrap the paper over the mixture to form a sausage shape. Twist the ends as tightly as you can (like a sweet wrapper) so that you have a solid log of butter. Refrigerate for 4 hours or overnight until firm.

Once firm, you can slice the butter into portions to use in cooking or to freeze for later use.

The Citrusy One

Especially good with poultry, pork, fish and seafood but also root vegetables, squashes, tofu, paneer and halloumi cheese.

VEGETARIAN

- **250g (9oz) salted butter, at room temperature**
- **1 heaped teaspoon sumac**
- **1 teaspoon paprika**
- **finely grated zest of 1 unwaxed lemon**
- **finely grated zest of 1 unwaxed orange**
- **finely grated zest of 1 unwaxed lime**
- **½ small packet (about 15g/½oz) of flat leaf parsley, finely chopped**
- **generous amount of freshly ground black pepper**

Put all the ingredients in a mixing bowl and stir together. Use a spatula to decant the mixture on to a piece of baking paper.

Wrap the paper over the mixture to form a sausage shape. Twist the ends as tightly as you can (like a sweet wrapper) so that you have a solid log of butter. Refrigerate for 4 hours or overnight until firm.

Once firm, you can slice the butter into portions to use in cooking or to freeze for later use.

The Sweetly Spiced One

VEGETARIAN

This makes a superb sweet and savoury addition to meats, but also try melting it in a pan to warm the dates through, then use to drizzle over sourdough toast, waffles or pancakes. This is also fantastic used as the butter element in loaf cakes, sticky toffee puddings or cookies!

- **250g (9oz) unsalted butter, at room temperature**
- **100g (3½oz) pitted dates, very finely chopped**
- **finely grated zest of 2 unwaxed oranges**
- **1 level teaspoon ground cinnamon**
- **1 teaspoon pul biber chilli flakes (optional)**

Put all the ingredients in a mixing bowl and stir together. Use a spatula to decant the mixture on to a piece of baking paper.

Wrap the paper over the mixture to form a sausage shape. Twist the ends as tightly as you can (like a sweet wrapper) so that you have a solid log of butter. Refrigerate for 4 hours or overnight until firm.

Once firm, you can slice the butter into portions to use in cooking or to freeze for later use.

Three Ways with… Pasta Sauce

Here are three quick, very different but utterly delicious pasta sauce recipes perfect for post-work dinners or quick meals any day of the week. They each serve two, but you can halve or double the quantities very easily.

Creamy Harissa

VEGETARIAN

Creamy, beautifully spiced and comforting – this is my go-to pasta sauce when I'm craving something simple yet satisfying.

SERVES 2

200g (7oz) spaghetti
1 tablespoon rose harissa
1 teaspoon garlic granules
5 tablespoons double cream
Maldon sea salt flakes and freshly ground black pepper

Cook the spaghetti in a large saucepan of boiling water according to the packet instructions until al dente. Drain, reserving some of the cooking water, and return to the pan.

Stir the harissa, garlic granules and cream into the cooked pasta in the pan and season generously with salt and pepper. Add enough of the reserved pasta water to create a sauce of your desired consistency and toss until evenly combined, then serve immediately.

GOES WELL WITH

The Really Useful Vegetable Traybake (see page 158).

Garlic Yogurt, Tahini & Dried Mint

VEGETARIAN

I love the comfort this recipe brings – the gentle tang of yogurt and crunch of pine nuts really makes it feel like a bowl of Eastern goodness.

SERVES 2

200g (7oz) spaghetti
250g (9oz) thick Greek yogurt (not Greek-style)
1 fat garlic clove, crushed
1 teaspoon tahini
1 teaspoon dried mint
Maldon sea salt flakes and freshly ground black pepper

To serve
2 spring onions, finely sliced
olive oil
½ teaspoon pul biber chilli flakes
a few toasted pine nuts

Cook the spaghetti in a large saucepan of boiling water according to the packet instructions until al dente. Drain, reserving some of the cooking water, and return to the pan.

While the pasta is cooking, mix all the main ingredients together in a bowl along with a generous amount of salt and pepper.

Add the yogurt mixture to the cooked pasta in the pan along with enough of the reserved pasta water to create a sauce of your desired consistency and toss until evenly combined. Stir through the spring onions and a drizzle of olive oil, then serve sprinkled with the pul biber and toasted pine nuts, and with a final grating of pepper.

GOES WELL WITH

The Really Useful Vegetable Traybake (see page 158).

Zhoug

VEGETARIAN & VEGAN

Arguably this could be a sort of Yemenite-style pesto, but make no mistake it's punchy, spicy, bold and delicious.

SERVES 2

200g (7oz) spaghetti
½ small packet (about 15g/½oz) of flat leaf parsley
½ small packet (about 15g/½oz) of fresh coriander
seeds from 2 green cardamom pods
1 green chilli
1 garlic clove
½ teaspoon ground cumin
½ teaspoon ground coriander
finely grated zest and juice of ½ unwaxed lemon
1 teaspoon sugar
olive oil
Maldon sea salt flakes and freshly ground black pepper

Cook the spaghetti in a large saucepan of boiling water according to the packet instructions until al dente. Drain, reserving some of the cooking water, and return to the pan.

While the pasta is cooking, blitz all the remaining ingredients in a small bullet blender or mini food processor, adding enough olive oil to achieve the consistency of a pesto.

Add the herb mixture to the cooked pasta in the pan along with enough of the reserved pasta water to slacken the sauce to your desired consistency and toss until evenly combined, then serve.

GOES WELL WITH
The Really Useful Vegetable Traybake (see page 158).

Three Ways with... Rice

The one thing people tell me most often is that they are afraid of cooking rice. But once you find a simple method and stick to it, it is actually really easy and the flavour combinations are endless. Here are three of my favourites.

Green Rice

VEGETARIAN & VEGAN

One of my childhood friends, Zyntya, first made this recipe for me when we were teens, and I have always remembered it. Years later I realized this green rice is a Mexican staple, and quite frankly it's absolutely delicious! This is my version made with basmati rice – so fragrant and flavourful, and a great one for pairing with so many dishes.

SERVES 3–4

300g (10½oz) basmati rice
450ml (16fl oz) cold water
4 fat garlic cloves
1 small packet (about 30g/1oz) of fresh coriander
1 small packet (about 30g/1oz) of flat-leaf parsley
1 heaped teaspoon garlic granules
1 tablespoon olive oil
Maldon sea salt flakes and freshly ground black pepper

Put the rice into a saucepan.

Blitz the cold water with the remaining ingredients along with a very heavy seasoning of salt and some pepper in a small bullet blender or mini food processor until completely smooth. Pour over the rice and stir to combine.

Place the saucepan over a medium heat (low if using a gas hob), cover the pan with a lid and cook for 30 minutes without stirring. Then turn off the heat and leave the rice to sit with the lid on for another 15 minutes. Fluff with a fork and serve.

GOES WELL WITH

Spicy Tomato Traybaked Chicken (see page 24).

Chickpea, Garlic, Cinnamon & Cumin Rice

VEGETARIAN

This dish takes some of the classic spices used in Middle Eastern rice dishes and pairs them with chickpeas to create a more substantial and fragrant side dish to any meal.

SERVES 3–4

olive oil
20g (¾oz) butter
4 fat garlic cloves, thinly sliced
400g (14oz) can chickpeas, drained
300g (10½oz) basmati rice
¼ teaspoon ground cinnamon
¼ teaspoon ground cumin
450ml (16fl oz) cold water
Maldon sea salt flakes and freshly ground black pepper

Place a saucepan over a medium-high heat, drizzle in a little olive oil and add the butter. Quickly add the garlic, so that the butter doesn't start to burn, and stir-fry until translucent and golden around the edges.

Add the chickpeas, rice and spices along with a heavy seasoning of salt and some pepper, then stir-fry for a couple of minutes.

Pour the cold water over the ingredients, stir briefly, then cover the pan with a lid and leave it to cook over a medium-high heat for 30 minutes – do not be tempted to stir the rice. Turn off the heat without removing the lid and leave to sit for 15 minutes, then fluff the rice with a fork and serve.

GOES WELL WITH

Nihari-style Lamb Shanks (see page 185) or Tangy Pomegranate Traybaked Chicken (see page 24) and Okra with Tomato & Garlic (see page 208).

Tomato, Ginger, Orange & Chilli Rice

VEGETARIAN

This spicy little number is a great accompaniment to many dishes, but I'll quite happily eat it with an egg cracked into a well in the rice for the last few minutes of cooking, then serve it with a little drizzle of sweet chilli sauce.

SERVES 3–4

finely grated zest and juice of 1 unwaxed orange
1 tablespoon olive oil
3 tablespoons tomato purée
1 teaspoon ginger purée/paste or 2.5cm (1 inch) piece of fresh root ginger, peeled and grated
1 teaspoon garlic granules
½ teaspoon chilli flakes
1 teaspoon dried oregano
25g (1oz) butter
300g (10½oz) basmati rice
Maldon sea salt flakes and freshly ground black pepper

Squeeze the juice of the orange into a measuring jug and top it up to 450ml (16fl oz) with cold water.

Place a saucepan over a medium heat, add the olive oil and then the tomato purée, ginger, orange zest, garlic granules, chilli flakes, oregano and butter and stir until the butter has melted. Add the rice and a very heavy seasoning of salt and some pepper and stir to coat in the mixture.

Pour the diluted orange juice over the rice mixture and stir well, breaking up any clumps of rice. Cover the pan with a lid and cook over a medium-high heat for 30 minutes. Turn the heat off and leave to sit without removing the lid for 15 minutes, then fluff with a fork and serve.

GOES WELL WITH

Juicy Joojeh Koobideh (see page 92).

Two Ways with... Traybaked Chicken

This is such a great method for cooking chicken. Slap a marinade on and rub it all over the chicken thighs – you can use drumsticks instead, if you like – then roast for about 40 minutes for perfect deliciousness every time. Needless to say, you can marinate the whole quantity of chicken and freeze half or simply halve the quantity from the start.

(SERVES 4–6)

1kg (2lb 4oz) bone in, skin-on chicken thighs

Maldon sea salt flakes and freshly ground black pepper

Spicy Tomato Marinade

4 tablespoons tomato purée

2 tablespoons olive oil

1 heaped tablespoon rose harissa

1 tablespoon garlic granules

1 tablespoon medium curry powder

2 teaspoons dried oregano

1 heaped teaspoon caster sugar

Tangy Pomegranate Marinade

3 tablespoons pomegranate molasses

2 tablespoons runny honey

1 tablespoon olive oil

1 level teaspoon ground cinnamon

Preheat the oven to 200°C, 180°C fan (400°F), Gas Mark 6. Line a large baking tray with baking paper.

Spread the chicken thighs out into a single layer, evenly spaced apart on the lined tray.

Mix the ingredients for your chosen marinade together in a small bowl along with a generous amount of salt and pepper until evenly combined. Rub the marinade over each piece of chicken to coat evenly and then bake for about 40 minutes until well browned and cooked through. Remove from the oven and serve.

GOES WELL WITH

Green Rice (see page 20) or Chickpea, Garlic, Cinnamon & Cumin Rice (see page 22).

Dips & Bits

Sometimes you just want a little something to snack on that is quick and tasty, or maybe you're planning a beautiful mezze spread or looking to add a few smaller dishes into a bigger feast. From dips and finger food, to snacks and easy midweek meals, you'll find plenty of ideas here.

Garlic & Potato Dip

I know what you're thinking… you're not sure if this works, but I'm here to tell you that it really does! Based on the Greek *skordalia*, this is a surprisingly wonderful dip that's great with a selection of toasted breads on the side, and you can even serve it as a side dish, too. Trust me, you need to try this one!

SERVES 4–6

750g (1lb 10oz) potatoes, peeled and quartered
olive oil
6 garlic cloves, crushed
75g (2¾oz) ground almonds
finely grated zest and juice of 1 unwaxed lemon
handful of chopped flat leaf parsley
3 spring onions, thinly sliced
1 teaspoon pul biber chilli flakes, plus extra to garnish
Maldon sea salt flakes and freshly ground black pepper

Cook the potatoes in a saucepan of boiling water, covered with a lid, for about 15 minutes or until cooked through. Drain and leave to cool.

Meanwhile, place the same pan over a medium heat, add a generous drizzle of olive oil, then add the garlic and ground almonds and mix well. Cook for a couple of minutes, stirring to avoid burning. Return the potatoes to the pan and mash with a potato masher or the end of a rolling pin. Add the lemon zest and juice, a generous amount of salt and pepper and a splash of water to help loosen the mixture, then stir really well. You want the mixture to be of a dipping consistency – I like to add quite a lot of olive oil to help achieve this which also contributes to that Mediterranean flavour.

Once you have your desired consistency, check and adjust the seasoning adding more salt or pepper as necessary. Remove from the heat and stir through the parsley, 2 of the chopped spring onions and the pul biber. Serve with a good drizzle of olive oil and an extra sprinkle of pul biber and the remaining spring onion.

GOES WELL WITH

Spiced Pear & Feta Salad with Watercress, Chicory & Pomegranate (see page 58) or Roasted Aubergine with Harissa Tomato Sauce & Mozzarella (see page 161).

Feta, Tarragon & Spice Rolls

These moreish, spiced little feta rolls tick all the boxes for me. Salty, spicy, creamy and delicious, they make a perfect quick snack and are great for sharing, too.

MAKES 16

200g (7oz) block of feta cheese, finely crumbled

4 spring onions, thinly sliced

1 teaspoon pul biber chilli flakes

½ teaspoon coarsely ground black pepper

1 heaped teaspoon dried dill

10g (¼oz) tarragon, leaves picked (about 2 handfuls of leaves) and finely chopped

1 x 320g (11¼oz) ready-rolled puff pastry sheet (about 350 x 230mm/14 x 9 inches)

1 egg, beaten

1 teaspoon nigella seeds

Preheat the oven to 220°C, 200°C fan (425°F), Gas Mark 7. Line a baking tray with baking paper.

Mix the feta, spring onions, spices and herbs together with a fork in a mixing bowl, keeping the mixture nice and crumbly.

Cut the pastry sheet lengthways into 4 equal long strips, then cut each strip into 4 rectangles.

Divide the feta mixture into 16 equal portions. Spread out one portion along one long edge of each pastry rectangle, then roll it up in the pastry to make a cigar shape.

Place the rolls on the lined tray, seam-side down. Brush them all over with the beaten egg and sprinkle with the nigella seeds, then bake for 20–22 minutes until golden brown. Remove from the oven and leave to cool slightly before eating.

GOES WELL WITH

Golden Spiced Parsnip Soup (see page 84) or Roasted Spiced Aubergine & Tomato with Yogurt & Herbs (see page 162).

Lazy Curried Cheese Mutabaq Toasties

All the best things are always wrapped in pastry or bread, in my humble opinion, and *mutabaq* is no exception. Literally meaning 'folded', these stuffed parcels are great carriers for absolutely any filling or leftovers. I've saved you the hassle of making a traditional bread dough and instead used a puff pastry sheet. You can easily halve the recipe, or vary the filling ingredients as you like.

MAKES 4

1 x 320g (11¼oz) ready-rolled puff pastry sheet (about 350 x 230mm/14 x 9 inches)

olive oil

For the filling

200g (7oz) feta, finely chopped

60g (2¼oz) mature Cheddar cheese, grated

2 spring onions, thinly sliced

generous handful of finely chopped fresh coriander

1 teaspoon chilli flakes

1 teaspoon medium curry powder

Maldon sea salt flakes and freshly ground black pepper

Cut the pastry sheet into 4 equal rectangles. Place one pastry rectangle between 2 sheets of baking paper and roll out as thinly as possible – don't worry about trying to make a perfect shape. Remove the top sheet of baking paper and set aside.

Mix the filling ingredients together in a bowl, season well, and divide into 4 equal portions. Spoon one portion into the centre of a pastry rectangle and spread it out to form a square shape. Carefully peel each edge of the pastry off the paper and fold over the filling into the centre to seal the filling and make a square parcel. Place the top sheet of baking paper back over and gently roll it flatter, but without applying full pressure to the rolling pin.

Repeat with the remaining pastry rectangles and filling portions.

Place a large nonstick frying pan over a medium heat and drizzle in a little olive oil. If using a gas hob, you need to be careful not to burn the pastry, so ensure you use a medium-low heat. Once the oil is hot, add the parcels seal-side up and cook for 6–8 minutes until browned and nicely crisped up on the underside. Rub a little olive oil over the uncooked side of the parcels, then carefully flip over and cook the undersides for 6–8 minutes. Remove from the pan and serve – be careful, as the cheese filling will be really hot!

GOES WELL WITH

Roasted Aubergine, Tomato, Pepper & Walnut Dip (see page 39), Tomato, Roasted Pepper & Harissa Soup (see page 83) or Green Beans with Tomato & Garlic (see page 204).

Feta & Herb Yogurt Dip

Now, before we proceed, let me just tell you that I can happily eat this entire dip by myself with a spoon, or even better, with bread – it is just so good and appeals to my garlic-loving nature. If you, too, love garlic, then this is for you. This recipe is based on a Persian dish called *maast o moosir*, meaning 'wild garlic yogurt'. Persian wild garlic is different to the leafy variety that we in the West know as wild garlic, so I've just used regular bulb garlic here and the result is almost exactly the same as the Persian original, but I've added some feta to the yogurt and finished with some extra flourishes, too. One thing I would emphasize is that you really need to ensure your garlic is very finely chopped rather than crushed or minced, otherwise it will be way too punchy. Serve with toasted bread like sourdough fingers or mini pittas, or even crudités. I could swim in this stuff, and it goes with everything, so you can serve it as part of any (and every) meal.

SERVES 4–6

500g (1lb 2oz) thick Greek yogurt
3 garlic cloves, very finely chopped
100g (3½oz) feta cheese, finely crumbled
finely grated zest of 1 unwaxed lemon or lime
a few mint leaves, rolled up tightly and thinly sliced into ribbons
small handful of dill, roughly chopped
½ teaspoon pul biber chilli flakes
olive oil
Maldon sea salt flakes and freshly ground black pepper

Mix the yogurt with the garlic and some salt and pepper in a bowl until well combined, but don't add too much salt, as the feta will also be salty. Add the feta and mix again. Leave the yogurt to sit for 30 minutes at room temperature – this is important so that the lactic acid in the yogurt has time to soften the kick of the garlic.

Mix the yogurt mixture before decanting on to a serving plate. Grate over the lemon or lime zest, sprinkle with the herbs and pul biber, and finish with a drizzle of olive oil to serve.

GOES WELL WITH

Ćevapčići (see page 88), Juicy Joojeh Koobideh (see page 92) or Firecracker Cauliflower Pilaf Traybake (see page 157).

Popcorn Aubergine

Usually anything fried popcorn-style gets my attention, and I love this method for cooking aubergine because it's so fast and makes it crisp and ever-so-poppable. It sounds weird but honey really works here, and a generous drizzle of your favourite chilli sauce and a squeeze of lime juice finishes it off perfectly. Alternatively, if you prefer a milder result, omit the honey and chilli sauce and drizzle with sweet chilli sauce instead.

SERVES 2–3

1 large aubergine, peeled and cut into 2cm (¾ inch) cubes
3 tablespoons cornflour
1 heaped teaspoon garlic granules
1 teaspoon paprika
vegetable oil
Maldon sea salt flakes

To serve
runny honey
sriracha or your favourite chilli sauce
1 lime, cut into 4 wedges

Put the aubergine, cornflour, garlic granules and paprika into a mixing bowl and then, using your hands, mix together well so that the aubergine absorbs the cornflour evenly.

Heat a large frying pan over a medium-high heat, pour in about 2.5cm (1 inch) vegetable oil and bring to frying temperature (add one of the aubergine cubes: if it sizzles immediately, the oil is hot enough). Line a plate with a double layer of kitchen paper. Add half the aubergine at a time to the hot oil and fry for a couple of minutes on each side, turning over gently with a slotted spoon, until deeply golden brown. Remove with the slotted spoon and transfer to the paper-lined plate to drain. Immediately season with salt.

Serve on a plate drizzled generously with honey and sriracha or other chill sauce, along with the lime wedges.

GOES WELL WITH

Spiced Pork & Pepper Traybake (see page 142) or Shuwa-style Lamb Shoulder (see page 189).

Roasted Aubergine, Tomato, Pepper & Walnut Dip

This is a phenomenally delicious dip that comes together with a simple tray-roasting of its key ingredients. The roasting process gives it a fresh but concentrated flavour, while the walnuts contribute some structure and texture, making it perfect for dipping into with toasted or warmed bread.

SERVES 4–6

- 1 large aubergine, peeled and cut into slices 1.5cm (⅝ inch) thick
- 2 large vine tomatoes, halved across the middle
- 1 large red pepper, cored, deseeded and cut into 6 pieces
- olive oil
- 100g (3½oz) walnuts
- 1 teaspoon cumin seeds
- 250g (9oz) thick Greek yogurt
- 2 garlic cloves, crushed
- ½ small packet (about 15g/½oz) of fat leaf parsley, finely chopped, some reserved for garnish
- juice of 1 lemon, to taste
- Maldon sea salt flakes and freshly ground black pepper
- toasted bread, to serve

Preheat the oven to 200°C, 180°C fan (400°F), Gas Mark 6. Line a large baking tray with baking paper.

Spread the vegetables out on the lined tray into a single layer and brush all their sides generously with olive oil. Roast for 30 minutes.

Remove from the oven, sprinkle over the walnuts and cumin and roast for another 6–7 minutes. Remove from the oven and leave to cool.

Transfer the cooled roasted veg mixture to a food processor and pulse until it forms a coarse dip consistency. Decant into a mixing bowl, add the yogurt, garlic, most of the parsley and a good squeeze of lemon juice. Drizzle over some olive oil, season generously with salt and pepper and mix well. Check the seasoning, adding more salt, pepper and lemon juice if needed, then garnish with more parsley, a final drizzle of olive oil and serve with toasted bread.

GOES WELL WITH

Khoresh e Aloo (see page 135) or Sweet & Spicy Spatchcocked Chicken (see page 176).

Curried Baby Corn & Spring Onion Beignets

I love baby corn, but I do feel it gets a bad rap, relegated to stir-fries and the odd Thai curry, and the worst crime of all, its random addition to a crudité platter. This recipe, in contrast, fully appreciates its texture and gentle sweetness, and moreover these fluffy, cloud-like beignets are kid-approved in that my sometimes-tricky sons like them. If that's not a green light to go and make them, I don't know what is!

MAKES 16–18

8 fat spring onions, thinly sliced
150g (5½oz) baby corn, thinly sliced into discs
1 heaped teaspoon mild curry powder
1 heaped teaspoon garlic granules
½ teaspoon ground turmeric
2 eggs
4 level tablespoons plain flour
½ level teaspoon baking powder
vegetable oil
Maldon sea salt flakes and freshly ground black pepper

To serve
sweet chilli sauce
lime wedges

Put all the main ingredients, except the oil, into a mixing bowl, season well with salt and pepper and stir until you have an evenly combined and smooth batter.

Heat a large frying pan over a high heat, pour in about 2.5cm (1 inch) vegetable oil and bring to frying temperature (add a little bit of the batter: if it sizzles immediately, the oil is hot enough). Line a large plate with a double layer of kitchen paper.

Stir the batter once again, then use a teaspoon to drop 16–18 beignets into the hot oil and fry for about a minute or so on each side, turning them over with a slotted spoon, until puffed up and deeply golden. Remove with the slotted spoon and transfer to the paper-lined plate to drain. Serve immediately with sweet chilli sauce and a good squeeze of lime juice.

GOES WELL WITH

Feta & Herb Yogurt Dip (see page 35) or Broken Eggs with Spiced Cannellini Beans (see page 106).

Labneh with Garlic, Tomatoes & Mint

My love for labneh knows no bounds and I thought I had exhausted the numerous ways in which to serve it, but this combo is new, inspired by a visit to a fantastic restaurant in Edinburgh named Baba. Making labneh couldn't be easier – you just need to allow time to leave some thick Greek yogurt to strain overnight. You can then add anything you like to it – just be sure to make those tomatoes good and garlicky!

SERVES 4–6

500g (1lb 2oz) thick Greek yogurt
1 teaspoon Maldon sea salt flakes
3 large tomatoes
2 garlic cloves, finely grated or minced
1 teaspoon pul biber chilli flakes
8 mint leaves, finely chopped
olive oil
freshly ground black pepper
toasted bread, to serve

The day before you want to serve this, season the yogurt with the salt and mix well, then spoon into a muslin cloth (or use a clean tea towel), gather the edges and tie tightly. Leave to strain over a bowl overnight in the refrigerator (I tie it to a wooden spoon, see overleaf), or if your kitchen is cool enough you can simply tie the bag to the kitchen tap and leave to drain over the sink.

The next day, remove the strained yogurt from the bag and smooth the contents on to a plate, or refrigerate to serve later.

Grate the tomatoes coarsely into a bowl, then decant into a fine-meshed sieve set over a small bowl to strain off the juice – don't shake the sieve, otherwise you will lose some of the pulp as well (drink the juice – it's delicious). Return the tomato pulp to the bowl, add the garlic and a good amount of salt and pepper and mix together, then pour over the labneh.

Sprinkle the dish with the pul biber, then finish with the mint and a generous drizzle of olive oil. Serve with your favourite toasted bread.

GOES WELL WITH

Chicken & Potato Traybake with Za'atar & Lemon (see page 148) or Shuwa-style Lamb Shoulder (see page 189).

Tomato, Feta & Garlic Toasts

Spanish *pan con tomate* is probably one of my favourite things to make at home whatever the time of year, even when tomatoes aren't in season – a little salt and pepper, some olive oil and a liberal application of garlic means it still has lots of flavour. This version makes it more of a meal, and tomatoes with feta are a match made in heaven. You can double this recipe very easily to share with friends, making triple or quadruple the quantity.

SERVES 1–2

a 10cm (3½in) length of ciabatta or baguette

1 small garlic clove

1 large ripe tomato (about 100g/3½oz)

25g (1oz) feta cheese, finely crumbled

good pinch of dried oregano

good pinch of pul biber chilli flakes

olive oil

Maldon sea salt flakes and freshly ground black pepper

Slice the ciabatta or baguette in half lengthways and toast until nicely browned. Rub the cut surfaces with the garlic clove, just enough to have kissed it... or if you, like me, love garlic, rub harder but be aware that the result will be very garlicky!

Grate the tomato coarsely into a bowl, then decant into a fine-meshed sieve set over a small bowl to strain off the juice – don't shake the sieve, otherwise you will lose some of the pulp as well (I like to season the tomato juice and drink it, as it's so delicious). Return the tomato pulp to the bowl, season well with salt and pepper and mix.

Divide the tomato between the 2 pieces of baguette, then sprinkle over the feta, oregano and pul biber and finish with a drizzle of olive oil. Enjoy!

GOES WELL WITH

Brilliant Breakfast Beans (see page 79).

Sweet Potato, Feta & Spring Onion Kuku

I love making *kuku*, and while I have created many other versions than the traditional herb, aubergine and potato varieties, each and every new combination brings me so much pleasure. This one is especially delicious, featuring gently sweet potatoes and creamy, salty feta – truly one of life's greatest pairings. While traditionally it would be fried, as with all my *kuku* recipes this version is baked for convenience, and you can serve it hot or cold.

SERVES 3–4

8 eggs
2 heaped tablespoons Greek-style yogurt
1 teaspoon baking powder
350g (12oz) sweet potatoes, peeled and cut into 1.5cm (⅝ inch) cubes
olive oil
4 spring onions, thinly sliced
200g (7oz) block of feta cheese, broken into small chunks
Maldon sea salt flakes and freshly ground black pepper

Preheat the oven to 220°C, 200°C fan (425°F), Gas Mark 7. Cut a large square of baking paper and scrunch it up, then smooth it out and use to line a 20cm (8 inch) square baking tin.

Put the eggs, yogurt, baking powder and a good amount of salt and pepper into a mixing bowl and lightly whisk with a fork until evenly combined and any baking powder lumps have dissolved.

Place the sweet potatoes in the lined tin, drizzle with olive oil and then rub it all over the potatoes. Season generously with salt and pepper and roast for 25 minutes until cooked through and soft. Remove from the oven and reduce the oven temperature to 200°C, 180°C fan (400°F), Gas Mark 6.

Scatter half the spring onions over the sweet potatoes, followed by all the feta and finally add the remaining spring onions. Carefully pour over the egg mixture, ensuring you distribute it evenly, and shake the tin so that the ingredients are mostly immersed in it. Bake for 25 minutes or until a knife inserted into the centre comes out clean (wet – yes, eggy – no). Remove from the oven and leave to cool slightly before enjoying.

GOES WELL WITH

Tangy Ottoman Orzo Salad (see page 64) or Roasted Spiced Aubergine & Tomato with Yogurt & Herbs (see page 162).

Spectacular Salads

I always say the best salads rarely involve lettuce! I've got all types of salads covered in this chapter, from lighter, fresher and zingy flavours to more comforting and substantial dishes, any of which would make an impressive part of a feast.

Spiced Beans with Herbs & Pomegranate

This is the kind of dish I absolutely love. It really has so much flavour, texture and vibrancy, and it's a very simple throw-together that looks wonderfully inviting. Perfect for sharing with friends and loved ones, it makes a great light lunch dish, if that's what you fancy. Any leftover dill and coriander stalks can be refrigerated or frozen for adding to soups and stocks.

SERVES 4–6

400g (14oz) can chickpeas, well drained

400g (14oz) can cannellini or butter beans, well drained

2 tablespoons olive oil

1 teaspoon ground turmeric

1 teaspoon ground cumin

1 teaspoon paprika

1 tablespoon garlic granules

Maldon sea salt flakes and freshly ground black pepper

For the salad

½ small packet (about 10g/¼oz) of chives, snipped into 2.5cm (1 inch) pieces

½ small packet (about 15g/1oz) of mint, leaves picked, rolled up tightly and thinly sliced into ribbons

½ small packet (about 15g/1oz) of dill, fronds picked

½ small packet (about 15g/1oz) of fresh coriander, leaves picked

150g (5½oz) baby plum tomatoes, quartered

75g (2¾oz) pomegranate seeds, some reserved for garnish

5 spring onions, thinly sliced diagonally

For the dressing

3–4 tablespoons Greek-style yogurt

3 tablespoons pomegranate molasses

Preheat the oven to 200°C, 180°C fan (400°F), Gas Mark 6. Line a large baking tray with baking paper.

Put the chickpeas and beans into a large mixing bowl, and add the olive oil, spices, garlic granules and a generous amount of salt and pepper, and mix together. Spread the mixture out on the lined tray into a single layer and roast for 35 minutes or so until lightly crisp. Remove from the oven and leave to cool, then tip out on to a large serving plate.

For the salad, toss together the herbs, tomatoes, pomegranate seeds and spring onions, then spoon on top of the chickpeas and beans.

For the dressing, thin the yogurt down with a tablespoon or so of cold water in a small bowl, season with salt and pepper and stir, then drizzle over the salad. Drizzle over the pomegranate molasses and the remaining pomegranate seeds, then serve.

GOES WELL WITH

Pomegranate Beef Short Ribs (see page 132) or Halloumi, Pepper & Spring Onion Tart (see page 165).

Punchy Prawn, Herb & Lime Lettuce Cups

I have always been a fan of meat or fish served in lettuce cups because it allows me to eat more, as the lettuce is a lighter carrier than bread. These spicy prawn cups don't even require the use of a saucepan or hob to make, only boiling water from a kettle to gently poach the prawns to perfection, so it's a winner for a quick snack or meal any time.

MAKES 8–10

250g (9oz) raw peeled prawns
2 fat spring onions, thinly sliced
½ small packet (about 15g/½oz) of mint, leaves finely chopped
½ small packet (about 15g/½oz) of fresh coriander, leaves finely chopped
1 heaped teaspoon pul biber chilli flakes
1 heaped teaspoon runny honey
finely grated zest and juice of 1 unwaxed lime
1 tablespoon olive oil
8–10 Baby Gem lettuce leaves
Maldon sea salt flakes and freshly ground black pepper

Put the prawns into a heatproof mixing bowl and pour over enough boiling water from a kettle to just cover them. Stir and leave them to sit immersed in the water for 1½ minutes until they turn fully opaque and pink. Drain the prawns and leave them to cool – they will still feel a little tender, but that's okay because the lime in the dressing will continue to 'cook' them and firm them up.

Once cool, roughly chop the prawns and return them to the bowl. Add all the remaining ingredients, except the lettuce, season with a generous amount of salt and pepper and mix well. Divide the mixture between the lettuce cups and serve.

GOES WELL WITH

Watermelon Salad with Toasted Rice & Tamarind Lime Dressing (see page 61), Carrot, Orange & Pepper Salad (see page 67) or Firecracker Cauliflower Pilaf Traybake (see page 157).

VEGETARIAN

Spiced Pear & Feta Salad with Watercress, Chicory & Pomegranate

I absolutely love fresh fruit in salads, especially pears with some peppery or bitter leaves. This is a really vibrant, colourful and delicious salad, laden with creamy feta and studded with juicy bursts of pomegranate seeds. It is especially good served with roasted meats and fish.

SERVES 4–6

- 3 pears, peeled, cored and cut into slices 5mm (¼ inch) thick
- 2 large heads of red or green chicory, leaves separated
- 150g (5½oz) watercress
- 100g (3½oz) feta cheese, very finely crumbled
- 50g (1¾oz) pecan nuts or walnuts, broken up by hand
- 100g (3½oz) pomegranate seeds

For the dressing

- 2 tablespoons olive oil
- 1 tablespoon runny honey
- finely grated zest and juice of 1 unwaxed lemon
- 1 teaspoon pul biber chilli flakes
- ½ teaspoon ground cinnamon
- Maldon sea salt flakes and freshly ground black pepper

Mix all the dressing ingredients together in a small bowl. Season well with salt and pepper, then set aside.

Arrange the pears, chicory leaves and watercress on a platter, then add the feta, pecan nuts or walnuts and pomegranate seeds. Drizzle the dressing over and serve.

GOES WELL WITH

Sweet & Spicy Spatchcocked Chicken (see page 176) or Marinated Steak Strips with Tomato Sauce & Garlic Yogurt (see page 180) or Sticky Roasted Salmon with Tamarind & Chilli (see page 189).

Watermelon Salad with Toasted Rice & Tamarind Lime Dressing

What the Thai don't know about creating explosive flavour combinations simply isn't worth knowing. I love making savoury salads that include fruit, and watermelon feels like the natural choice for a Persian girl like me, but this salad is somewhat influenced by my love of Thai salads and the addition of toasted rice really makes it. This is fantastic with grilled meats and fish.

SERVES 3–4

- **1 teaspoon uncooked basmati or jasmine rice**
- **500g (1lb 2oz) watermelon, peeled, any seeds removed and cut into small bite-sized pieces**
- **1 large or 2 small long (banana) shallots, thinly sliced into rings, or 1 small red onion, halved and thinly sliced into half moons**
- **3 springs onions, thinly sliced diagonally**
- **generous handful of mint leaves, rolled up tightly and thinly sliced into ribbons**
- **⅓ small packet (about 10g/½oz) of fresh coriander, finely chopped**

For the dressing

- **finely grated zest and juice of 1 unwaxed lime**
- **1 tablespoon caster sugar**
- **1 heaped teaspoon pul biber chilli flakes**
- **1 teaspoon tamarind paste**
- **1 teaspoon light soy sauce**
- **1 teaspoon olive oil**
- **Maldon sea salt flakes and freshly ground black pepper**

Heat a dry frying pan over a medium-high heat, add the rice and toast, shaking the pan occasionally, for 2 minutes, or until the rice is deep golden brown, but not burnt. Remove from the heat and leave to cool. Using a pestle and mortar, grind the toasted rice as finely as you can until you reach the consistency of coarse sand grains. Don't be tempted to use a spice or coffee grinder, as it will produce way too fine a powder.

For the dressing, whisk the lime zest and juice and sugar together with a fork in a small bowl until the sugar has dissolved. Then add the remaining dressing ingredients, season with salt and pepper and mix well.

Mix all the salad ingredients together in a large bowl, pour the dressing over and mix again until evenly dressed. Sprinkle with the toasted rice and serve.

GOES WELL WITH

Punchy Prawn, Herb & Lime Lettuce Cups (see page 57) or Sticky Roasted Salmon with Tamarind & Chilli (see page 189).

Sweetcorn & Feta Pasta Salad

A classic tuna pasta salad remains one of my all-time favourite salad recipes, holding strong nostalgic links to my childhood, and it's something I make for my family regularly today. But my tuna-hating husband doesn't partake, so this is an alternative version featuring feta and Cheddar instead that we all love.

SERVES 4–6

250g (9oz) mini pasta shells or any other shape (such as ditalini or margheritine soup pasta)

2 sweetcorn cobs, kernels sliced off with a knife

200g (7oz) block of feta cheese, finely crumbled

150g (5½oz) mature Cheddar cheese, grated

6 spring onions, thinly sliced

1 red pepper, cored, deseeded and finely chopped

2 fat garlic cloves, crushed

2 heaped teaspoons pul biber chilli flakes

finely grated zest of 1 large unwaxed lime and juice of ½

5 tablespoons mayonnaise (I prefer to use a light version)

1 small packet (about 30g/1oz) of fresh coriander, finely chopped

Maldon sea salt flakes and freshly ground black pepper

Cook the pasta, together with the sweetcorn kernels, in a saucepan of boiling water according to the packet instructions. Drain and rinse thoroughly in a sieve under cold water, then drain again and set aside for a few minutes to dry.

Transfer the pasta and sweetcorn to a large bowl, add all the remaining ingredients with a generous seasoning of salt and pepper and stir together gently, then serve.

GOES WELL WITH

Spicy Orange Chicken Bites (see page 95) or Mango, Lime & Chilli Chicken (see page 146).

Tangy Ottoman Orzo Salad

While not an authentic dish, I'd like to think that if the Ottomans created a pasta salad, this would be it. With all the familiar flavours of Turkish *kısır* and a few extra gems thrown in, this is a pasta salad like no other and I absolutely love it and hope you will, too. It's perfect alongside roasted or grilled meat and fish, and any leftovers are great for a lunchbox.

SERVES 4–6

250g (9oz) orzo pasta
150g (5½oz) pitted Kalamata olives, halved
250g (9oz) semi-dried tomatoes in oil, each tomato snipped into 4 pieces, some oil reserved for dressing
1 small packet (about 30g/1oz) of flat leaf parsley, finely chopped
1 small red onion, finely chopped
1 red pepper, cored, deseeded and finely chopped
150g (5½oz) pomegranate seeds
2 tablespoons tomato purée
2 tablespoons pomegranate molasses
2 heaped teaspoons pul biber chilli flakes
1 heaped teaspoon paprika
1 heaped teaspoon dried oregano
Maldon sea salt flakes and freshly ground black pepper

Cook the orzo in a large saucepan of boiling water according to the packet instructions. Drain and rinse thoroughly in a sieve under cold water, then drain again.

Transfer the orzo to a large bowl, add all the remaining ingredients and stir. Season with salt and pepper, stir again, then serve.

GOES WELL WITH

Ćevapčići (see page 88), Juicy Joojeh Koobideh (see page 92) or Shuwa-style Lamb Shoulder (see page 189).

Carrot, Orange & Pepper Salad

This salad is a lovely option for the less sunny months when you're in need of something crunchy and vibrant. It's a juicy little number that is perfectly refreshing and great on its own, but also makes a good accompaniment to any meal.

SERVES 4–6

4 large carrots, peeled

3 small oranges, peeled and segmented

1 red onion, halved and thinly sliced into half moons

100g (3½oz) pomegranate seeds

½ red pepper, cored, deseeded and very thinly sliced

½ yellow pepper, cored, deseeded and very thinly sliced

½ small packet (about 15g/½oz) of mint, leaves picked, rolled up tightly and thinly sliced into ribbons

For the dressing

1 tablespoon pomegranate molasses

1 teaspoon pul biber chilli flakes

½ teaspoon ground cinnamon

olive oil

Maldon sea salt flakes and freshly ground black pepper

Cut each carrot into 2–3 equal lengths, thinly slice, then cut each slice into thin matchsticks. If you have one, a julienne disc on a food processor will do the job easily, but I like doing it by hand.

Put the prepared carrots into a large bowl with all the remaining salad ingredients and mix together, then decant on to a serving platter.

Put the dressing ingredients in a small bowl and add some salt, pepper and a light drizzle of olive oil and stir until well combined. Drizzle over the salad and lightly toss before serving.

GOES WELL WITH

Mango, Lime & Chilli Chicken (see page 146) or Sticky Roasted Salmon with Tamarind & Chilli (see page 189).

Green Bean, Broccoli & Potato Salad with Pickled Chillies & Preserved Lemons

This is a very simple salad that is a real pleasure to eat. It has a dressing, of sorts – the flavourings come from the salad ingredients: salt from the capers, sour from the preserved lemons and heat from the pickled chillies. When they're all mixed together with plenty of olive oil and a little seasoning, this makes for a delicious dish. And if you're looking to make more of a meal of this recipe, try adding some tuna chunks or diced feta cheese.

SERVES 4–6

- **500g (1lb 2oz) new potatoes**
- **200g (7oz) trimmed extra-fine green beans**
- **200g (7oz) Tenderstem broccoli**
- **4 red pickled chillies, thinly sliced (seeds and all)**
- **3 preserved lemons, deseeded and thinly sliced into half moons**
- **2 heaped tablespoons capers**
- **olive oil**
- **Maldon sea salt flakes and freshly ground black pepper**

Cook the potatoes in a saucepan of boiling water for 15–20 minutes until cooked through. Drain and leave just until cool enough to handle, then cut each into 3–4 slices.

Place the green beans and Tenderstem broccoli in a microwaveable bowl, cover with a lid or clingfilm and cook in a microwave on a high power for 3–4 minutes. Alternatively, steam them in a colander over a pan of boiling water. Just don't boil them, as you will lose their goodness and flavour.

Put the pickled chillies, preserved lemons and capers into a large bowl with 3 tablespoons olive oil and some salt and pepper and mix until well combined. Add the warm potatoes, beans and broccoli and stir together well. Leave the salad to sit for 10 minutes, then check and adjust the seasoning if desired, and add a little more olive oil if needed before serving.

GOES WELL WITH

Ćevapčići (see page 88), Juicy Joojeh Koobideh (see page 92), Sweet & Spicy Spatchcocked Chicken (see page 176) or Marinated Steak Strips with Tomato Sauce & Garlic Yogurt (see page 180).

Apple, Lentil, Ginger & Cranberry Rice Salad

I love a good salad. And when I say 'good', I usually mean one that's substantial enough to be eaten on its own. This is a great mix of flavours that are really refreshing, but also easy to throw together. It's a very versatile dish, as you can use any rice you like and any dried fruit you have. Halve the quantities if you wish, or just enjoy the leftovers – if there are any!

SERVES 6–8

200g (7oz) basmati rice
2 large sweet apples, cored and cut into small cubes
100g (3½oz) dried cranberries
1 red onion, very finely chopped
400g (14oz) can green lentils, drained and rinsed

For the dressing
1 small packet (about 30g/1oz) of fresh coriander
1 small packet (about 30g/1oz) of flat leaf parsley
2 teaspoons ginger purée/paste or 5cm (2 inch) piece of fresh root ginger, peeled and grated
juice of ½ lemon
3 tablespoons olive oil
2 tablespoons red wine vinegar
2 tablespoons runny honey
2 teaspoons pul biber chilli flakes
Maldon sea salt flakes and freshly ground black pepper

Cook the rice in a saucepan of water according to the packet instructions. Drain and rinse thoroughly in a sieve under cold water. Drain thoroughly by shaking the sieve, then set aside.

Blitz all the dressing ingredients, except the honey and pul biber, with a generous seasoning of salt and pepper in a small bullet blender or mini food processor until as smooth as possible. Decant into a large mixing bowl, add the honey and pul biber and mix well.

Add the apples, cranberries and onion to the bowl and stir to coat in the dressing. Add the lentils and cooked rice and fold into the mixture. Check and adjust the seasoning, adding more salt and pepper as needed, then stir again before serving.

GOES WELL WITH

Mango, Lime & Chilli Chicken (see page 146) or Sticky Roasted Salmon with Tamarind & Chilli (see page 189).

Kamounit Banadoura

This is a dish that I just can't get enough of, and I often wonder how something so simple can be so delicious? It really is mind-boggling. But what's more puzzling for me is how to explain exactly what this is to people from the West. It's not a dip, it's almost a salad – it's a dish that can be eaten with bread along with raw onion 'petals' (my favourite way to enjoy it, as it greatly satisfies my Persian desire for raw onion). The recipe hails from southern Lebanon and it was very much love at first bite when I tried it, so I felt compelled to share it with you. The one thing I must stress is that you really do need to hunt down fine bulgur wheat for this recipe, which isn't the kind you usually find in supermarkets, but if you have to use regular bulgur, then add more liquid by way of tomatoes, warm water and lemon juice, and adjust the flavourings accordingly.

SERVES 6–8

- 3 large tomatoes, 2 very finely chopped
- 2 small onions, 1 very finely chopped
- 200g (7oz) fine bulgur wheat (not the regular coarse kind!)
- 1 small packet (about 30g/1oz) of mint, leaves picked
- 1 small packet (about 30g/1oz) of basil, leaves picked
- 1 teaspoon cumin seeds
- juice of 1 lemon
- 1 heaped tablespoon tomato purée
- 1 heaped teaspoon dried mint
- 1 teaspoon ground cinnamon
- olive oil
- Maldon sea salt flakes and freshly ground black pepper

To serve

- flatbreads
- 2 red onions, quartered, with the layers split into 'petals'

Put the 2 very finely chopped tomatoes and 1 very finely chopped onion into a mixing bowl and set aside.

Add all the remaining main ingredients to a food processor with a generous glug of olive oil (3–4 tablespoons or enough to make the mixture spin) and a very generous seasoning of salt and pepper. Blitz the mixture right down until everything is evenly blended and smooth.

Decant the mixture into the bowl with the tomatoes and onion and mix together well, then check and adjust the seasoning. Serve on a platter with an extra drizzle of olive oil along with some flatbreads and the quartered red onion petals to scoop up the mixture.

GOES WELL WITH

Nihari-style Lamb Shanks (see page 185) or Shuwa-style Lamb Shoulder (see page 189).

Pasta Salad Olivieh

Every time I roast a whole chicken, I pick over the carcass for the leftover meat, and this is one of the dishes I love making with it. I had to figure out a way to sneak this into the book, because I've started making this twist on a Persian salad *olivieh* (based on the Russian classic potato-based salad) using pasta instead of potatoes and, dear reader, it is rather marvellous. But how does it fit in with my concept of only cooking in one vessel? Well, you can of course cook the eggs, pasta and peas separately or, if you're lazy like me, you can do it all in one pot! It's absolute magic and a real time/washing-up/energy saver.

SERVES 6

250g (9oz) pasta shapes, such as farfalle or conchiglie

4 medium or large eggs

3 large handfuls of frozen peas

200–250g (7–9oz) leftover roast chicken meat, or 2 cooked chicken breasts, skin removed and finely chopped

150g (5½oz) large pickled cucumbers, finely chopped

250g (9oz) mayonnaise (I prefer to use a light version)

juice of ½ lemon

Maldon sea salt flakes and freshly ground black pepper

Bring a saucepan of water to the boil and check the packet instructions to see how long your pasta needs cooking, depending on its shape and size (usually 8–12 minutes). You will then need to boil your eggs for 8 minutes if medium or 9–10 minutes if large, and the peas for 2–3 minutes. So first add your pasta to the boiling water, then your eggs, then your peas, setting a timer for the appropriate timings. Once everything is cooked, drain and rinse thoroughly in a sieve under cold water, then drain again, shaking off the excess water.

Put the chicken, pickles, mayonnaise and lemon juice into a large mixing bowl. Shell the eggs and finely chop them, then add to the bowl along with the pasta and peas. Season generously with salt and pepper and mix everything together until evenly combined and coated in the mayonnaise. Check and adjust the seasoning adding more salt and pepper if desired, before serving. This needs no accompaniment.

Easy Everyday

This chapter features recipes for any time of the week... quick, satisfying and delicious, and extra easy for those occasions when speed and simplicity is much needed.

Brilliant Breakfast Beans

Beans are a staple breakfast in much of the Middle East and North Africa, and there are so many delicious versions from region to region and country to country that it's easy to understand why they are so loved. This spiced version is very much my own, and the kind of dish that you serve in the pan on the table for everyone to share. You can even crack eggs into it to poach gently or serve with eggs cooked your favourite way, but I love it best with flatbread, scooped straight from the pan. This dish is perfect for breakfast, and also for lunch or dinner.

SERVES 2–3

olive oil
1 onion, finely chopped
3 fat garlic cloves, finely chopped
½ teaspoon chilli flakes
½ teaspoon ground cumin
½ teaspoon ground coriander
½ teaspoon ground turmeric
1 large tomato, finely chopped
1 heaped teaspoon tomato purée
400g (14oz) can borlotti beans, drained
handful of chopped flat leaf parsley or fresh coriander leaves, finely chopped, to serve

For the tahini yogurt
100g (3½oz) thick Greek yogurt
1 tablespoon tahini
Maldon sea salt flakes and freshly ground black pepper

For the tahini yogurt, mix the yogurt, tahini and some salt and pepper together in a bowl, adding enough lukewarm water to thin it down to a dollop-able consistency. Set aside.

Place a frying pan over a medium heat, drizzle in enough olive oil to coat the base and cook the onion until translucent and golden brown at the edges. Add the garlic and spices and stir well, then add the tomato and tomato purée along with a few tablespoons of warm water. Mix everything well, cover the pan with a lid and cook for a few minutes.

Add the beans followed by a generous amount of salt and pepper and stir to coat the beans in the onion and spice mixture. Add 3 more tablespoons of warm water and stir again. Replace the lid and cook for 10 minutes, stirring occasionally to prevent sticking.

Remove the lid and stir – lightly mash some of the beans as you do. Check the seasoning and stir in a little more water, if desired. Spoon the tahini yogurt on top in the centre and smooth over, drizzle with olive oil, then serve sprinkled with the parsley or coriander to finish.

GOES WELL WITH

Feta, Tarragon & Spice Rolls (see page 31) or Tomato, Feta & Garlic Toasts (see page 47).

VEGETARIAN

Ultimate Sunday Brunch Smash

This is everything I could possibly want to eat for brunch (or lunch or dinner, for that matter) all in one pan. It's an explosion of flavour and makes me very happy indeed, especially with some good bread to dip into it. It's creamy, salty, oozy, spicy, zingy and sweet – something for everyone. You can be sure it will be your new favourite brunch dish!

SERVES 2–4

1 tablespoon rose harissa

olive oil

250g (9oz) halloumi cheese, cut into 4 slices and each slice cut into 6 cubes (24 cubes in total)

4 eggs

2 fat spring onions, thinly sliced diagonally

about 1 heaped teaspoon runny honey

Maldon sea salt flakes and freshly ground black pepper

tortilla wraps, to serve

For the lime & herb yogurt

150g (5½oz) thick Greek yogurt

1 fat garlic clove, minced or crushed

finely grated zest of 1 unwaxed lime and juice of ½

½ packet (about 15g/1oz) of dill, finely chopped, a little reserved for garnish

½ packet (about 15g/1oz) of fresh coriander, finely chopped, a little reserved for garnish

drizzle of olive oil

Mix all the yogurt ingredients together in a bowl along with some salt and pepper until well combined, then set aside.

Mix the harissa with 1 teaspoon of olive oil in a cup and set aside.

Place a nonstick frying pan over a medium-high heat. Add 2 tablespoons olive oil. Once hot, add the halloumi cubes and fry for a few minutes on 2 sides until deeply golden brown. Make 4 wells in the halloumi and crack an egg into each. Cover the pan with a lid and cook for 3–4 minutes until the whites are completely opaque, then remove from the heat.

Keeping the eggs in the pan, season with a little salt and pepper, dollop with the yogurt and dot with the harissa oil, then sprinkle with the spring onions and the reserved herbs. Drizzle with the honey and serve with tortilla wraps.

GOES WELL WITH

Feta, Tarragon & Spice Rolls (see page 31) or Green Beans with Tomato & Garlic (see page 204).

Tomato, Roasted Pepper & Harissa Soup

Soups are a staple in my house and what I love about this one is that it's largely made from my store-cupboard essentials. The only fresh ingredients you need are the onions and garlic, and you're on your way to a bowl of comfort in next to no time. Serve with crusty bread or chargrilled bread rubbed with garlic and olive oil.

SERVES 3–4

olive oil
2 brown onions, roughly chopped
6 fat garlic cloves, bashed, peeled and left whole
2 x 400g (14oz) cans chopped tomatoes
450g (1lb) jar roasted red peppers in brine, drained and roughly chopped (remove any blackened skin)
1 heaped teaspoon paprika
2 tablespoons tomato ketchup
2 tablespoons rose harissa
1 heaped teaspoon caster sugar
1 vegetable stock pot or cube
Maldon sea salt flakes and freshly ground black pepper
toasted bread rubbed with garlic and olive oil, to serve

Place a large saucepan over a medium-high heat, pour in enough olive oil to coat the base generously and cook the onions and garlic for 6–8 minutes, stirring occasionally, until softened and translucent but without colouring more than golden brown. Add the canned tomatoes, peppers, paprika, ketchup, harissa, sugar, stock pot or cube and a generous amount of salt and pepper, stir well and cook for 5 minutes.

Pour over enough boiling water from a kettle to barely cover all the ingredients, reduce the heat to medium and stir again. Cover the pan with a lid and cook for 30 minutes. Check that your onions and garlic are soft, and if not, replace the lid and cook for another 15 minutes. Remove from the heat and then, using a stick blender, blitz the soup until completely smooth.

Return to the heat, then check and adjust the seasoning if desired and add more water if needed. Heat through before serving.

GOES WELL WITH

Feta, Tarragon & Spice Rolls (see page 31) or Lazy Curried Cheese Mutabaq Toasties (see page 32).

Golden Spiced Parsnip Soup

Why parsnips seem to be confined to being eaten only at Christmas, I'll never know! They are one of my favourite vegetables and their natural sweetness means they are a perfect pairing with spice. This soup is so comforting and packed full of flavour, and uses the aroma and flavour of fresh turmeric and a little curry powder to transform it into something truly special. Serve with lots of crusty bread and enjoy.

SERVES 4–6

olive oil
2 large onions, roughly chopped
50g (1¾oz) fresh turmeric, scrubbed and chopped
1 head of garlic, cloves separated, bashed and peeled
1kg (2lb 4oz) parsnips, peeled and roughly chopped
1 tablespoon medium curry powder
juice of ½ fat lime
Maldon sea salt flakes and freshly ground black pepper

Place a large saucepan over a medium-high heat, drizzle in some olive oil and cook the onions, turmeric and garlic for 5 minutes, stirring occasionally but not letting them brown. Add the parsnips, curry powder and a generous amount of salt and pepper, stir well and cook for another 5 minutes, then add about 100ml (3½fl oz) warm water to lift the spice from the base of the pan and prevent anything from sticking or burning. Cook the ingredients for a further 5 minutes or so, stirring occasionally to ensure they don't colour.

Pour over enough boiling water from a kettle to cover the ingredients, reduce the heat to medium and cook, uncovered, for 45 minutes.

Remove from the heat and, using a stick blender, blitz the soup until smooth. Return to the heat, squeeze in the lime juice and stir. Check and adjust the seasoning if desired and add more water if needed. Heat through before serving.

GOES WELL WITH

Feta, Tarragon & Spice Rolls (see page 31) or Tomato, Feta & Garlic Toasts (see page 47).

Keema Spiced Filo Pan Pie

This is simple to make, the filling can be varied and with a little cheeky/sneaky wiping can be prepared all in the one pan, with less fuss and less washing-up. You can use either lamb or beef – the result is equally delicious, so the choice is entirely yours and I hope that flexibility gives you one more reason to make it.

SERVES 2–4

olive oil
1 onion, very finely chopped
250g (9oz) minced lamb or beef
1 teaspoon garlic granules
½ teaspoon ground turmeric
¼ teaspoon ground cloves
¼ teaspoon ground cinnamon
¼ teaspoon chilli flakes
1 tablespoon tomato purée
generous handful of frozen peas
4 sheets of filo pastry (each about 480 x 250mm/19 x 10 inches)
Maldon sea salt flakes and freshly ground black pepper

Place a large frying pan over a medium-high heat, drizzle in enough olive oil to coat the base and fry the onion for 8–10 minutes until nicely browned but not burned. Add the minced meat and fry, breaking it up as finely as you can to prevent it cooking in clumps. While still uncooked, add the garlic granules, all the spices and a generous amount of salt and pepper and stir regularly until cooked.

Stir in the tomato purée until evenly combined, then mix in the frozen peas. Check and adjust the seasoning, adding more salt and pepper if desired, then transfer the meat mixture to a plate.

Wipe the pan clean with some kitchen paper and place the pan over a medium heat.

Lay 2 filo pastry sheets on your work surface and brush them with olive oil. Place one sheet on top of the other, to form a cross. Place the pastry oil-side down in the pan, leaving the edges overhanging. Add the meat mixture on top of the filo and spread it out in an even layer.

Oil the 2 remaining sheets of filo and again, layer them on top of each other to form a cross. Lay the pastry, oil side up, on top of the meat and tuck the edges snugly around the meat. Fold the overhanging filo over the top of the pie. Brush the top with a little olive oil, and cook for 6–8 minutes.

Place a plate over the pan and carefully flip the pan over to turn the pie out on to the plate. Slide the pie back into the pan and cook the underside for 5–6 minutes before serving.

GOES WELL WITH

Roasted Spiced Aubergine & Tomato with Yogurt & Herbs (see page 162) or Pomegranate Sweet Potatoes (see page 168).

Ćevapčići

Ćevapčići (or _ćevapi_) are popular throughout the Balkans in slightly differing forms. These little sausage-like koftas are the treats from my childhood, when I spent a few summers in Germany with my aunt and she introduced me to a canned version of ćevapčići that came on a bed of rice. One bite and I was hooked! Years later, I started thinking about them again, and while I truly miss their flavour, adult-me wanted to create my own fresh and more grown-up version inspired by those summer days of my childhood.

MAKES 16

1 large onion
250g (9oz) minced pork, 20% fat
250g (9oz) minced beef, 20% fat
4 fat garlic cloves, crushed
1 heaped tablespoon dried oregano
1 tablespoon paprika
¼ teaspoon bicarbonate of soda
¼ teaspoon chilli flakes
vegetable oil
Maldon sea salt flakes and freshly ground black pepper

To serve
flatbreads
sliced onions
Greek yogurt
chilli sauce (optional)

Blitz the onion in a small bullet blender or mini food processor until finely minced and its juices have been released.

Transfer the onion to a mixing bowl and add all the remaining main ingredients, except the oil, along with a generous amount of salt and pepper. Using your hands, work the ingredients together really well for a few minutes until you have a smooth and evenly combined paste. Divide the mixture into 16 equal portions and carefully roll into balls, then roll each ball into a sausage shape to create the ćevapčići.

Heat a large frying pan over a medium-high heat and add a generous drizzle of vegetable oil. Cook half the ćevapčići for 3–4 minutes on each side until deeply browned. To ensure the remaining edges are browned, cook for another couple of minutes while shaking the pan frequently.

Remove the cooked ćevapčići to a plate and cover with foil to keep warm, then cook the remainder. Serve with flatbreads, sliced onions and a little yogurt, along with chilli sauce if desired.

GOES WELL WITH
Feta & Herb Yogurt Dip (see page 35) or My-style Batata Harra (see page 154).

Sticky Honey, Lime & Harissa Sausage Meatballs

Sausages are a great staple in many family homes, and I often use sausagemeat in pastas, wraps and more. These little sausage meatballs are sticky, sweet, spicy and delicious, and one of the easiest dishes to cook. This is my favourite way to eat them – in a baguette, or *banh mi*-style with some fresh coriander and crunchy pickled carrot. They are also great in mini wraps or with steamed rice. Whatever you serve them with, this is a recipe you really need to try, and the family will love them.

SERVES 3–4

450–500g (1lb–1lb 2oz) sausagemeat
2 tablespoons runny honey
1 heaped tablespoon rose harissa
juice of ½ fat lime
Maldon sea salt flakes

To serve
baguettes or cooked rice
2 spring onions, thinly sliced

Divide the sausagemeat into 16 equal portions and roll each into a ball.

Heat a dry frying pan over a medium-high heat, add the sausage meatballs (without adding oil, as they will quickly release their fat) and fry for 3–4 minutes on each side until firm and well browned. To ensure the remaining edges are browned, cook for another couple of minutes while shaking the pan frequently.

Meanwhile, mix the honey, harissa and lime juice together in a small bowl.

Increase the heat under the pan to high, add the honey mixture and turn the meatballs until evenly coated and the sauce begins to thicken and evaporate. Keep moving the meatballs and coating them until nicely glazed. Serve in baguettes or with rice, sprinkled with the spring onions.

GOES WELL WITH
Traybaked Ludicrously Good Latke (see page 171) or Sweet Pickled Broccoli & Cauliflower Stir-fry (see page 211).

Juicy Joojeh Koobideh

Persians love their *kabab koobideh*, a minced meat *kabab* usually made with lamb, but in the last couple of decades minced chicken has become more and more popular. This easy version is inspired by *koobideh*, but the flavours are all my own, and even better, you are spared the fiddly rolling and shaping of them here, as it's all done in the baking tray!

MAKES 8

1 large onion
500g (1lb 2oz) minced chicken thighs (not lean)
1 heaped teaspoon garlic granules
1 heaped teaspoon pul biber chilli flakes
1 teaspoon ground turmeric
1 teaspoon dried oregano
¼ teaspoon bicarbonate of soda
olive oil spray or olive oil
Maldon sea salt flakes and freshly ground black pepper

To serve
sliced onions
pickled cucumbers
thick Greek yogurt
chilli sauce
flatbreads

Preheat your oven to its highest setting (with fan if it has one). Line a baking tray with baking paper.

Blitz the onion in a small bullet blender or mini food processor until finely minced and its juices have been released.

Decant the onion into a large mixing bowl and add all the remaining main ingredients, except the oil, along with plenty of salt and pepper. Using your hands, work the ingredients together really well for a few minutes until you have a smooth and evenly combined paste.

Tip out the mixture on the lined tray and form it into one big rectangular shape about 1.5cm (¾ inch) thick. Using a spatula or a flat-bladed knife to push the mixture apart, split the mixture lengthways in half, then cut each half into 4 long kebabs (8 in total). Dampen your little finger with water then make diagonal indentations for a traditional appearance.

If you have an oil spray, spray the kebabs with olive oil, or brush the exposed surfaces with oil using a pastry brush, then roast for 12 minutes. Remove from the oven and serve with sliced onions, pickled cucumbers, yogurt, your favourite chilli sauce and flatbreads.

GOES WELL WITH
Three Ways With Rice (see pages 20–3), Tangy Ottoman Orzo Salad (see page 64) or My-style Batata Harra (see page 154).

Spicy Orange Chicken Bites

This method is an absolute lifesaver – no-mess, fuss-free chicken thighs cooked in around 20 minutes. Despite the high heat, the chicken remains juicy and tender, and it's great for serving with tortilla wraps to soak up all that juicy goodness. But I also like spooning all the pan juices over rice or potatoes to serve. You can easily halve the recipe below, if you wish, but leftovers are the gift that keeps on giving.

SERVES 4–6

800g–1kg (1lb 12oz–2lb 4oz) boneless, skinless chicken thighs, each cut into bite-sized pieces

For the marinade

2 tablespoons rose harissa

2 heaped tablespoons runny honey

finely grated zest and juice of 1 orange

1 tablespoon garlic granules

Maldon sea salt flakes and freshly ground black pepper

Preheat your oven to its highest setting (with fan if it has one). Line a large baking tray with baking paper.

Put the chicken pieces on the lined tray. Add the marinade ingredients directly to the chicken, along with some salt and pepper. Using your hands, mix everything together, then spread out the chicken pieces so they sit snugly together in one layer. Roast for 18–20 minutes.

Remove from the oven and baste the chicken with the juices, then roast for another 5–7 minutes (depending on how high your oven temperature goes) until nicely charred on outside. Remove from the oven and serve with the juices spooned over.

GOES WELL WITH

Three Ways with Rice (see pages 20–3) or Spiced Beans with Herbs & Pomegranate (see page 52).

Prawn, Ginger & Tomato Fry

I make this sort of dish all the time. You can't really call it a curry because the ingredients aren't traditional, but it's quick, delicious and very useful for midweek meals or surprise visitors! This is great served on mini tortilla wraps or with some basmati rice.

SERVES 2–3

olive oil
50g (1¾oz) fresh root ginger, peeled and cut into very thin matchsticks
2 garlic cloves, finely chopped
1 heaped tablespoon rose harissa
1 teaspoon medium curry powder
400g (14oz) can chopped tomatoes
1 teaspoon caster sugar
250g (9oz) frozen raw peeled prawns, defrosted and patted with kitchen paper, or fresh
handful of chopped fresh coriander
Maldon sea salt flakes and freshly ground black pepper

Place a frying pan over a medium heat, drizzle in some olive oil and stir-fry the ginger for a few minutes until it softens – if using a gas hob, add a little water to help prevent the ginger from sticking to the pan and burning. Add the garlic and stir-fry until golden, but don't let either ingredient colour any further, as they will turn bitter.

Add the harissa and curry powder and mix well, then pour in the canned tomatoes and season with a generous amount of salt and pepper and the sugar. Stir really well and simmer for 15–20 minutes or so until reduced, stirring occasionally to prevent burning.

Increase the heat and cook for a few more minutes, stirring well, then add the prawns and cook for 2–3 minutes until they turn fully opaque and pink and are firm to the touch. Sprinkle with the coriander, then serve.

GOES WELL WITH

Three Ways with Rice (see pages 20–3) or Pomegranate Sweet Potatoes (see page 168).

Cod, Sweet Potato, Pepper & Black-eyed Bean Stew

One of my favourite ways to eat fish is when it's cooked in some kind of sauce, whether in a stew or curry, the sauce safely delivering that flavour boost some people feel fish needs. This is a meal in itself, being hearty, flavoursome and delicious, and needs no accompaniment, but of course you can serve it with anything you like. Perfect for sharing or you can happily halve the recipe, too.

SERVES 4

olive oil

500g (1lb 2oz) sweet potatoes, peeled and cut into about 1.5cm (⅝ inch) cubes

1 teaspoon garlic granules

1 heaped teaspoon pul biber chilli flakes

1 teaspoon paprika

1 teaspoon ground coriander

½ teaspoon ground turmeric

1 red pepper, cored and deseeded, and thinly sliced

400g (14oz) can black-eyed beans, drained

400g (14oz) can chopped tomatoes

400g (14oz) skinless cod loin or fillet, cut into bite-sized chunks

Maldon sea salt flakes and freshly ground black pepper

handful of chopped flat leaf parsley or fresh coriander, to serve

Place a large frying pan over a medium-high heat and drizzle in a generous amount of olive oil. Add the sweet potatoes and garlic granules along with all the spices and stir well to coat the potatoes in the oil and flavourings, then cook for a few minutes.

Add the red pepper and cook for 5 minutes, then stir in 2–3 tablespoons of water. Cover the pan with a lid and cook for 5 minutes, shaking the pan occasionally to prevent sticking.

Remove the lid, stir in the beans and cook for 5 minutes. Next, add the canned tomatoes and a very generous amount of salt and pepper and stir well. Replace the lid and cook for 15 minutes, again shaking the pan occasionally.

Remove the lid, check the seasoning and add more salt and pepper if needed, then stir again. Add the cod and gently coat it in the sauce and other ingredients, then replace the lid and cook for 6–7 minutes until the fish is firm and opaque. Stir gently, sprinkle with the parsley or coriander, then serve.

GOES WELL WITH

Feta & Herb Yogurt Dip (see page 35) or Spiced Pear & Feta Salad with Watercress, Chicory & Pomegranate (see page 58).

Cod with Herby Orzo & Green Beans

This is my one-pan comfort food of dreams. Not only is it a fantastically fuss-free way to cook fish, but this packs in veggies and carbs with a dreamy, creamy, herby sauce that is really satisfying. You can also use salmon instead of the cod if you prefer.

SERVES 2–3

olive oil
1 small onion, very finely chopped
100g (3½oz) orzo pasta
500ml (18fl oz) boiling water
50g (1¾oz) fine green beans, trimmed and halved
1 teaspoon garlic granules
100ml (3½fl oz) double cream
250g (9oz) skinless cod loin, cut into big chunks
4 fat spring onions, diagonally cut into 1cm (½ inch) pieces
handful of tarragon leaves, roughly chopped
handful of dill, fronds roughly chopped
Maldon sea salt flakes and freshly ground black pepper

Place a large frying pan over a medium-high heat, add enough olive oil to coat the base and fry the onion until translucent. Add the orzo and stir to coat it in the oil and onion mixture, then reduce the heat to medium and cook for 5 minutes.

Pour the boiling water over and gently simmer, stirring occasionally, for 8–10 minutes until firmly al dente – the exact timing will depend on the orzo, so check for doneness at 8 minutes.

Add the green beans, a generous amount of salt and pepper and more water if needed and stir well, then cook for 3–4 minutes. Stir in the garlic granules and cream and then place the fish pieces on top. Cover the pan with a lid and cook for 5 minutes.

Remove the lid, stir in the spring onions and check and adjust the seasoning according to your preference, then add the herbs and stir through the dish. Add a little more water if desired and serve. Don't worry about breaking the fish up – it's fine and makes for a very delicious end result. This needs no accompaniment.

Nutty Harissa Egg Kari

When I come home tired, anything with eggs is a quick fix, so I find myself turning to them time and time again. This dish looks and tastes indulgent, as if it's taken much longer to make when actually it can be ready in just 10 minutes. So for me, this is a really satisfying and delicious dish to throw together. Serve with flatbreads or on top of jasmine or basmati rice.

SERVES 2

4 medium or large eggs
2 heaped tablespoons crunchy or smooth peanut butter (I like crunchy)
1 heaped teaspoon rose harissa
½ teaspoon caster sugar
6–8 tablespoons milk
Maldon sea salt flakes

To serve
2 spring onions, thinly sliced
small handful of fresh coriander, roughly chopped

Bring a medium-sized saucepan of water to the boil, add the eggs and cook for 8 minutes if medium or 9–10 minutes if large, then drain and plunge into cold water. Shell the eggs and cut in half.

Wipe out the pan and place over a medium heat. Add the peanut butter, harissa, sugar and some salt and mix well. The mixture will thicken quickly, so use the milk to thin it down to a sauce-like consistency that will serve 2 people. If you don't want to measure the quantity, just add a little milk a spoonful at a time until the consistency is gravy-like.

Heat the sauce through, then add the egg halves and stir to briefly coat in the sauce. Spoon out on to a serving plate and serve topped with the spring onions and coriander.

GOES WELL WITH

Three Ways with Rice (see pages 20–3) or The Really Useful Vegetable Traybake (see page 158).

Broken Eggs with Spiced Cannellini Beans

Broken eggs are my new thing, and I'm not entirely certain if this is a bean dish or more of an omelette. What I can tell you is that this recipe for garlicky fried beans with eggs cracked on top and lightly stirred in to create a mix of yolk, white and bean is very satisfying indeed. You can serve it directly in the cooking pan and it's great for breakfast, lunch or dinner, especially with some toasted crusty bread.

SERVES 2–4

olive oil

4 garlic cloves, finely chopped

½ teaspoon ground cumin

½ teaspoon ground coriander

½ teaspoon chilli flakes, plus extra to serve

400g (14oz) can cannellini beans, drained

⅓ small packet (about10g/¼oz) of flat leaf parsley, finely chopped, a little reserved for garnish

4 eggs

Maldon sea salt flakes and freshly ground black pepper

Place a large nonstick frying pan over a medium heat and drizzle in a generous amount of olive oil, then add the garlic and stir well. Cook for a couple of minutes, stirring occasionally, and then add the spices, stir well and cook for another couple of minutes.

Add the beans and stir carefully to coat them with the garlic mixture. Season generously with salt and pepper and cook for a couple of minutes, then add the parsley and stir again.

Crack the eggs on to the beans, break into the yolks and very lightly and only briefly mix into the beans. Cook until the egg whites are opaque and cooked through, then serve immediately topped with the reserved parsley and a good sprinkle of chilli flakes.

GOES WELL WITH

Roasted Aubergine with Harissa Tomato Sauce & Mozzarella (see page 161) or Roasted Spiced Aubergine & Tomato with Yogurt & Herbs (see page 162).

Spaghetti with Oregano, Lemon & Pul Biber

This is a clever yet simple pasta dish made all in one pot for maximum flavour and minimal washing-up. It's quick, easy and absolutely delicious, making it a perfect midweek go-to.

SERVES 2

200g (7oz) spaghetti
olive oil
25g (1oz) butter
3 fat garlic cloves, very finely chopped
½ teaspoon dried oregano
finely grated zest of 1 unwaxed lemon and juice of ½
75ml (2½fl oz) double cream
50g (1¾oz) Parmesan cheese, freshly grated
½ teaspoon pul biber chilli flakes
Maldon sea salt flakes and freshly ground black pepper

Cook the spaghetti in a large saucepan of boiling water according to the packet instructions until al dente. Scoop out about 400ml (14fl oz) of the cooking water into a measuring jug and set aside.

Drain the pasta of the remaining cooking water, return it to the pan and place over a medium-high heat. Add a little drizzle of olive oil, the butter and garlic, then toss the pasta for 30 seconds.

Gradually stir in the reserved pasta water in batches – it should absorb pretty quickly, so keep stirring and add just enough of the water until it creates a starchy creamy sauce, then add the oregano, lemon zest and juice, a heavy seasoning of pepper and salt to taste.

Stir vigorously until the sauce thickens, then add the cream and Parmesan and mix quickly together to ensure the cheese melts into the sauce, adding a little more pasta water if needed. Finally, add the pul biber, stir through, then serve. This needs no accompaniment.

Mushroom, Garlic & Paprika Orzo

This is a deceptively simple dish that delivers big, comforting flavour. When you eat it, a stroganoff may spring to mind, and that's very much intended. A perfect, indulgent yet meat-free midweek meal.

SERVES 2–3

250g (9oz) chestnut mushrooms, halved and thickly sliced
olive oil
4 fat garlic cloves, thinly sliced
200g (7oz) orzo pasta
400–450ml (14–16fl oz) boiling water (depending on the orzo you use)
2 teaspoons paprika
1 teaspoon garlic granules
1 tablespoon light soy sauce
100ml (3½fl oz) double cream
Maldon sea salt flakes and freshly ground black pepper
handful of thinly sliced chives, to serve (optional)

Heat a dry saucepan over a high heat, add the mushrooms and cook for a few minutes, stirring occasionally, until all their liquid has been released and evaporated and they have browned a little. Transfer to a plate and set aside.

Reduce the heat under the pan to medium, then drizzle in enough olive oil to coat the base, add the garlic and stir quickly to prevent burning. Add the orzo and stir to coat with the garlic and oil. Pour in 400ml (14fl oz) boiling water (you can add more later, if needed), stir and cook for about 10 minutes, stirring occasionally to prevent sticking. Test the orzo: if cooked to your liking, add the paprika, garlic granules, soy sauce and a generous amount of salt and pepper and stir well. If the orzo isn't quite cooked, add the extra 50ml (2fl oz) boiling water and cook until done, then add the flavourings.

Return the mushrooms to the pan, then stir in the cream. Check and adjust the seasoning, adding more salt and pepper if desired, then serve sprinkled with the chives, if using. This needs no accompaniment.

Halloumi, Coconut & Black Bean Stew

Sometimes you need something really comforting but quick, and as halloumi, canned beans and coconut cream are house staples for me, throwing them together with a little spice seemed a very natural thing to do. This gently spiced stew could almost be a curry, and the soft, almost quivering texture of the halloumi is really lovely – it offers plenty of reward in very little time. Serve with flatbreads or potatoes, or this is also great with rice or grains of your choice.

SERVES 2–3

- olive oil
- 1 large onion, halved and thinly sliced into half moons
- 4 fat garlic cloves, thinly sliced
- 1 heaped teaspoon garlic granules
- 1 heaped teaspoon paprika
- 1 heaped teaspoon ground turmeric
- ½ teaspoon chilli flakes
- 400g (14oz) can black beans, drained and rinsed
- 250ml (9fl oz) coconut cream
- 250g (9oz) block of halloumi cheese, cut into very small cubes
- Maldon sea salt flakes and freshly ground black pepper

Place a saucepan over a medium heat, drizzle in some olive oil and cook the onion for a few minutes until softened and translucent. Add the garlic and cook for a minute, then stir in the garlic granules and spices and cook for 2 minutes.

Stir in 2 tablespoons of warm water, just to lift the spices from the base of the pan and prevent burning, then stir in the beans and cook for 5 minutes, stirring regularly. Add the coconut cream and a generous amount of salt and pepper, stir well and cook for a further 5 minutes.

Add the halloumi, stirring, increase the heat to medium-high and cook for 10–12 minutes until the cheese is nice and soft, then serve.

GOES WELL WITH

Three Ways with Rice (see pages 20–3), Pomegranate Sweet Potatoes (see page 168) or Okra with Tomato & Garlic (see page 208).

Weekend Wonders

For times when you want to make a big batch of something and eat-on-repeat or share with friends and family. This chapter contains lots of fantastic ideas for soups, stews and slow cooks to make your weekend more wonderful!

Meatball Fesenjan

I do love a good *fesenjan* (Persian walnut, pomegranate and chicken stew), and my classic recipe resides in my first book *Persiana*, but this is a quick and easy version using meatballs – a popular alternative to chicken and my favourite as a kid. Because you don't need to slow-cook this version, it's ready in less than half the time. Serve it with basmati rice.

SERVES 4–6

200g (7oz) walnuts
500g (1lb 2oz) minced lamb or beef (15–20% fat)
vegetable oil
1 large onion, very finely chopped
1 teaspoon ground turmeric
200ml (7fl oz) warm water, plus another 200ml (7fl oz)
200ml (7fl oz) pomegranate molasses
3 tablespoons caster sugar

Blitz the walnuts in a food processor until ground as finely as possible, then set aside.

Roll the minced meat into 36–40 mini meatballs and set aside.

Place a large saucepan over a medium-high heat, drizzle in enough vegetable oil to coat the base and cook the onion for a few minutes until softened and translucent. Add the turmeric and ground walnuts, reduce the heat to medium and cook for 10 minutes, stirring regularly to prevent burning. Pour in the 200ml (7fl oz) warm water, stir really well and cook for 10 minutes, stirring regularly.

Add the pomegranate molasses, sugar and the remaining 200ml (7fl oz) warm water, stir well and cook for 5 minutes until the sugar has dissolved. Add the meatballs and gently shake the pan to immerse them in the sauce without stirring – until they are cooked they will be soft and will easily crumble apart. Reduce the heat to low and cook for 30–40 minutes, stirring gently but regularly once the meatballs are firm to prevent burning, until the liquid reduces and thickens, then serve.

GOES WELL WITH
Chickpea, Garlic, Cinnamon & Cumin Rice (see page 22) or Spiced Pear & Feta Salad with Watercress, Chicory & Pomegranate (see page 58).

Moroccan Harira

This is more than just a soup. Harira is the comforting bowl of nourishment that you never knew you needed. It's hearty, warmly spiced and it's absolutely delicious. While traditionally made with meat, you can ditch it in favour of a plant-based alternative. Either way, the combination of spices, pulses and rice makes for a stunning dish that is also very easy to make and feeds a crowd. But equally, once cooked, you can freeze half, or simply make half the quantity.

SERVES 4–6

olive oil

2 onions, halved and thinly sliced into half moons

1 large carrot, peeled and finely chopped

500g (1lb 2oz) lamb neck fillets, cut into small dice

1 head of garlic, cloves separated, peeled and thinly sliced

500g (1lb 2oz) ripe tomatoes, roughly chopped

3 tablespoons tomato purée

1 teaspoon ground cumin

1 teaspoon ground ginger

1 teaspoon ground turmeric

1 teaspoon paprika

75g (2¾oz) uncooked green lentils

400g (14oz) can chickpeas, including the liquid from the can

100g (3½oz) basmati rice

1 small packet (about 30g/1oz) of fresh coriander, finely chopped

1 small packet (about 30g/1oz) of flat leaf parsley, finely chopped

Maldon sea salt flakes and freshly ground black pepper

lemon wedges, to serve (optional)

Place a large saucepan over a medium-high heat, pour in enough olive oil to generously coat the base and fry the onions and carrot, stirring, until softened. Add the lamb, garlic, tomatoes, tomato purée, spices and a generous amount of salt and pepper, stir well and cook for 5–6 minutes.

Add enough boiling water from a kettle to generously cover the ingredients, cover the pan with a lid and cook for 1¼ hours, stirring occasionally to prevent burning.

Stir in the lentils and the chickpeas with their liquid, stir and top up the liquid level with boiling water. Replace the lid and cook for another 30 minutes, stirring occasionally.

Add the rice and stir well, then cook for a final 15 minutes, uncovered, until tender. Check and adjust the seasoning, then stir through most of the herbs, sprinkle over the remainder to garnish and serve with lemon wedges if desired. This needs no accompaniment.

Shami Kofta

Shamis are a favourite in many cultures, from South Asia to Iran and the Middle East. Minced lamb mixed with mashed chickpeas makes for smooth and soft koftas that feel lighter. I think poaching them in a spicy tomato sauce is such a good way to make them and avoids having to fry them first. Diving straight into the pan with flatbreads is a very pleasing way to enjoy this dish, but it's also great with basmati rice or potatoes.

SERVES 4–6

olive oil
6 large garlic cloves, thinly sliced
1 heaped tablespoon rose harissa
2 x 400g (14oz) cans chopped tomatoes
1 heaped teaspoon caster sugar
400g (14oz) can chickpeas, drained
1 large onion, quartered
500g (1lb 2oz) minced lamb (minimum 20% fat)
1 tablespoon garlic granules
1 heaped teaspoon ground turmeric
1 teaspoon ground cumin
Maldon sea salt flakes and freshly ground black pepper

Place a large saucepan over a medium heat, drizzle in enough olive oil to coat the base and cook the garlic for a few minutes until translucent. Stir the harissa into the garlic and fry for a minute. Add the canned tomatoes, sugar and a generous amount of salt and pepper and cook for about 10 minutes, stirring occasionally, while you make your koftas.

Blitz the chickpeas and onion together in a food processor until they form a paste that is as smooth as possible. Transfer to a large mixing bowl, then add the minced lamb, garlic granules, spices and a generous amount of salt and pepper to the mixture. Using your hands, work the ingredients together really well for a few minutes until you have a smooth and evenly combined paste.

Divide the mixture into 20–22 equal portions and roll into small sausage shapes, then add them into the sauce – nestle them snugly next to each other, without stirring, as they will be soft and may easily crumble. Cover the pan with a lid ,reduce the heat to low and cook for 30 minutes, by which time they will become firm, and you can give them a careful stir. Cook for a further 10–15 minutes, uncovered, to reduce the sauce before serving.

GOES WELL WITH

Chickpea, Garlic, Cinnamon & Cumin Rice (see page 22), Green Beans with Tomato & Garlic (see page 204) or Okra with Tomato & Garlic (see page 208).

Lamb & Pistachio Khoresh

This is a lesser-known Persian stew that deserves to be celebrated more. What I love about Persian stews (*khoresh*) is that essentially they are fairly simple in flavour profile, being usually either herb- or tomato-based, so this is a wonderfully easy recipe to make. Traditionally we would always serve it with basmati rice, but you can enjoy it with whatever you like.

SERVES 5–6

100g (3½oz) pistachio nuts (I use green, skinless pistachio slivers)

vegetable oil

2 onions, finely chopped

750g (1lb 10oz) lamb neck fillets, split lengthways and cut into 2cm (¾ inch) chunks

½ teaspoon ground turmeric

1 small packet (about 30g/1oz) of fresh coriander, finely chopped

1 small packet (about 30g/1oz) of flat leaf parsley, finely chopped

Maldon sea salt flakes and freshly ground black pepper

Blitz the pistachios in a mini food processor until ground as finely possible, then set aside.

Place a large saucepan over a medium-high heat and pour in enough vegetable oil to generously coat the base. Once hot, add the onions and cook for 8–10 minutes until translucent but without colouring.

Add the lamb, turmeric, herbs and a generous amount of salt and pepper and mix well, then cook for about 10 minutes until the herbs turn dark green and look like very well-cooked spinach.

Stir in the ground pistachios and pour over enough water to barely cover the ingredients. Reduce the heat to medium-low, cover the pan with a lid and gently simmer for 2 hours, stirring every 20 minutes or so to ensure the pistachios don't burn on the base of the pan. Remove the lid, and if you want to reduce the liquid then increase the heat and stir regularly until reduced. Serve and enjoy.

GOES WELL WITH

Feta & Herb Yogurt Dip (see page 35) or Spiced Pear & Feta Salad with Watercress, Chicory & Pomegranate (see page 58).

Lamb, Harissa & Chickpea Tagine

Everything about these flavour combinations reminds me of Morocco, though it's fair to say that this is not a remotely traditional combination, but rather an amalgamation of feel-good flavours that are quick to throw together for a pretty spectacular result. Sweet, spicy, meaty and comforting, there's a little hit of pleasure to satisfy every taste bud. It works well with bread or rice, couscous or bulgur wheat.

SERVES 3–4

olive oil
2 large onions, halved and thinly sliced into half moons
500g (1lb 2oz) lamb neck fillets, cut into slices 2.5cm (1 inch) thick
1 large head of garlic, cloves separated, bashed and peeled
2 heaped tablespoons rose harissa
2 teaspoons paprika
1 heaped teaspoon ground cumin
1 heaped teaspoon ground ginger
1 teaspoon ground turmeric
2 large peppers (I used red and yellow), cored, deseeded and sliced into 3cm (1 inch) thick strips
400g (14oz) can chickpeas, drained
2 tablespoons runny honey
juice of ½ fat lemon
large handful of dried apricots
Maldon sea salt flakes and freshly ground black pepper

To serve
handful of toasted nuts (I use flaked almonds)
handful of flat leaf parsley, roughly chopped

Place a large saucepan over a medium-high heat, drizzle in enough olive oil to coat the base, then cook the onions for a few minutes until softened but no more than just golden around the edges. Add the lamb, whole garlic cloves, harissa, spices and a generous amount of salt and pepper and stir well. Reduce the heat to medium and cook, stirring occasionally, for 5 minutes.

Pour over enough boiling water from a kettle to cover the meat and cook, uncovered, for an hour, stirring occasionally to prevent burning. Check the liquid level and top up with boiling water if needed.

Add the peppers, chickpeas, honey and lemon juice, stir well and cook for another 30 minutes. Stir in the apricots and cook for a final 30 minutes, stirring regularly. Check and adjust the seasoning, adding more salt and pepper if needed, before serving with the toasted nuts and parsley on top.

GOES WELL WITH

Three Ways with Rice (see pages 20–3) or Pomegranate Sweet Potatoes (see page 168).

Swahili-style Lamb Stew

I originally intended this recipe to be a Swahili-style biryani, but having made that, the meat and sauce was so delicious in itself that I felt obliged to turn it into a much simpler stew version, without the traditional large quantity of separate crispy fried onions. This is great served just with flatbreads or with basmati rice, and it freezes beautifully, too.

SERVES 3–4

- **vegetable oil**
- **1 large onion, very finely chopped**
- **6 large garlic cloves, bashed and peeled**
- **500g (1lb 2oz) lamb neck fillets, split lengthways and cut into 2.5cm (1 inch) cubes**
- **seeds from 6 fat green cardamom pods, ground using a pestle and mortar**
- **2 teaspoons ground cumin**
- **1 teaspoon ground turmeric**
- **1 teaspoon ground cinnamon**
- **½ teaspoon ground cloves**
- **2 heaped tablespoons tomato purée**
- **400g (14oz) can chopped tomatoes**
- **350g (12oz) small potatoes, peeled and cut into slices 1.5cm (⅝ inch) thick**
- **150g (5½oz) Greek-style yogurt**
- **Maldon sea salt flakes and freshly ground black pepper**

Place a saucepan over a high heat and pour in enough vegetable oil to generously coat the base. Once hot, add the onion and fry for 8–10 minutes until the onion is browning around the edges. Add the garlic, followed by the lamb and cook, stirring occasionally, for 8–10 minutes until browned.

Add all the spices, tomato purée and a generous amount of salt and pepper and mix well to coat the lamb evenly, then cook for 5 or so minutes. Next, stir in the canned tomatoes, potatoes and yogurt until combined. Reduce the heat to medium, cover the pan with a lid and cook for 1½ hours, stirring regularly to prevent burning.

Remove the lid and check and adjust the seasoning if desired, then cook, uncovered, for 30 minutes to reduce the liquid. Check that the meat is tender and if necessary cook for a little longer before serving.

GOES WELL WITH

Carrot, Orange & Pepper Salad (see page 67), Green Beans with Tomato & Garlic (see page 204) or Okra with Tomato & Garlic (see page 208).

Saffron Vermicelli with Koftas

If you like paella, then you need to try its Catalan cousin *fideuà* – a dish that uses vermicelli instead of rice as the main ingredient. It's much lighter and I absolutely love it, and my humble recipe here pays homage to this dish but with a Middle Eastern twist. The use of saffron in both paella and *fideuà* gives Persian-me so much pleasure; in addition I've introduced my own element in the form of family-friendly koftas, making it perfect for everyone. While the recipe is easy to halve, I'd happily eat this for three days in a row on my own!

SERVES 4–6

500g (1lb 2oz) minced beef or lamb (15–20% fat)
olive oil
1 large onion, finely chopped
6 fat garlic cloves, thinly sliced
a generous pinch of saffron
1 large red pepper, cored, deseeded and finely chopped
200g (7oz) broken egg vermicelli
lemon wedges, to serve

For the stock

500ml (18fl oz) boiling water
1 chicken or vegetable stock pot or cube
2 tablespoons tomato purée
Maldon sea salt flakes and freshly ground black pepper

Roll the minced meat into 36–40 mini meatballs and set aside.

Place a large, deep frying pan over a medium-high heat, drizzle in enough olive oil to coat the base and cook the onion for a few minutes until it begins to brown around the edges. Add the garlic, saffron and red pepper and cook for 5 minutes, stirring occasionally. Stir in the vermicelli strands for a couple of minutes until coated in the mixture, then add the meatballs.

For the stock, pour the boiling water into a measuring jug, add the stock pot or cube and tomato purée along with a generous amount of salt and pepper and stir until dissolved. Pour over the ingredients in the pan and stir briefly – be careful as the meatballs will be soft and easily crumble before they are cooked.

Reduce the heat to medium, shake the pan gently to level the ingredients out and cover with a lid. Cook for 20 minutes, then turn off the heat and leave to sit without removing the lid for 10 minutes. Remove the lid and serve with lemon wedges.

GOES WELL WITH

Roasted Spiced Aubergine & Tomato with Yogurt & Herbs (see page 162) or Green Beans with Tomato & Garlic (see page 204).

Pomegranate Beef Short Ribs

Considering all the cuts of beef, I must say that shin, brisket and ribs are my favourite – I just love how tender they become after being cooked slowly. This is a delicious way to prepare beef short ribs, in a reduced sauce which becomes really flavourful and hits every taste bud and all the high notes on the satisfaction scale. And if you want to make this dish go further, you can easily add a couple of extra ribs to the pot, just as long as it's big enough to fit them in! Serve with mash or roast potatoes, or pull the meat and serve it in flatbreads.

SERVES 2–4

- **4 large beef short ribs (about 3kg/6lb 8oz total weight)**
- **150ml (5fl oz) pomegranate molasses**
- **1 teaspoon chilli flakes**
- **1 teaspoon paprika**
- **1 teaspoon ground cinnamon**
- **2 tablespoons light brown soft sugar**
- **1 heaped tablespoon tomato purée**
- **Maldon sea salt flakes and freshly ground black pepper**

Heat a large deep saucepan over a medium-high heat and sear the short ribs on both the fat and meat side for a few minutes until nicely browned. You can discard the rendered fat if you wish, but to be honest I never do.

Mix all the remaining ingredients together in a measuring jug, add a generous amount of salt and pepper, then dilute with some hot water from a kettle and pour over the beef ribs. Pour more boiling water into the pan – just enough to barely cover the ribs. Cover the pan with a lid, reduce the heat to a medium simmer and cook for 3½ hours, turning the ribs over a few times and ensuring there is enough liquid to cook them.

Remove the lid, then lift out the ribs on to a plate and cover with foil to keep warm while you finish the sauce. The bones will most likely have detached themselves from the meat, which is a great sign, so just discard them – you can also shred the meat if you want to. Increase the heat under the pan to high and cook the sauce, stirring occasionally, until it reaches a thicker consistency (you can continue to reduce the sauce until it becomes a sticky glaze, if desired), then pour over the ribs and serve.

GOES WELL WITH

Firecracker Cauliflower Pilaf Traybake (see page 157) or Baked Sweet Potatoes with Yogurt, Harissa & Chives (see page 172).

Khoresh e Aloo

For every fruit and vegetable that grows in Iran, there is a stew to match. Plum stew is traditionally made with lamb and dried Bukhara plums, but I love adding my own twist and using fresh plums and chicken instead. The classic dish is undeniably delicious, but this version of mine is very worthy of being shared, too. Also, this freezes really well. You can serve it with flatbreads or basmati rice.

SERVES 3–4

vegetable oil
1 large onion, finely chopped
1 small packet (about 30g/1oz) of flat leaf parsley, finely chopped
1 small packet (about 30g/1oz) of fresh coriander, finely chopped
600–650g (1lb 5oz–1lb 7oz) boneless, skinless chicken thighs
1 teaspoon ground turmeric
1 heaped tablespoon tomato purée
4 large plums, stoned and halved
Maldon sea salt flakes and freshly ground black pepper

Place a saucepan over a medium-high heat, drizzle in enough vegetable oil to coat the base and cook the onion until softened and translucent. Add the herbs and cook them for about 10 minutes until they turn dark green and look like well-cooked spinach.

Add the chicken, turmeric and tomato purée, stir well and cook for another 10 minutes, stirring occasionally. Season generously with salt and pepper, then reduce the heat to medium, pour over enough water to barely cover the ingredients and stir. Cook, uncovered, for 1 hour, stirring occasionally to prevent burning.

Check and adjust the seasoning, then add the plum halves and ensure they are just about immersed in liquid. Cook for another 15–20 minutes, stirring occasionally and adding a splash more water to keep the plums immersed if necessary. The dish is ready when the plums are soft but remain whole and the chicken is tender.

GOES WELL WITH

Chickpea, Garlic, Cinnamon & Cumin Rice (see page 22) or Roasted Aubergine, Tomato, Pepper & Walnut Dip (see page 39).

Aunty Souri's Tamarind Aash

Given that my mother never (ever) cooked, I always felt incredibly lucky to have Aunty Souri in my life. When I was a kid, she cooked delicious home-cooked meals that felt so special every time. Nowadays, when my mum comes home from spending quality time with Aunty Souri, she always sings the praises of one particular dish – her tamarind *aash*, so much so that I called Aunty Souri and asked her for a recipe, which I'm pleased to share with you here.

SERVES 3–4

olive oil
2 onions, finely chopped
4 fat garlic cloves, thinly sliced
100g (3½oz) flat leaf parsley, finely chopped (stalks and all)
100g (3½oz) fresh coriander, finely chopped (stalks and all)
3 tablespoons dried dill
100g (3½oz) uncooked red lentils
2 tablespoons tomato purée
1 heaped tablespoon tamarind paste
400g (14oz) can borlotti beans, including the liquid from the can
Maldon sea salt flakes and freshly ground black pepper

Place a saucepan over a medium heat, drizzle in enough olive oil to coat the base and cook the onions and garlic for a few minutes until translucent. Add the fresh herbs, dried dill and a generous amount of salt and pepper, stir well and cook for 20 minutes or so, stirring occasionally to prevent them sticking to the pan – you can add a small cup of water to prevent the herbs sticking, but you need to cook them until they go dark and resemble well-cooked spinach.

Stir in the lentils and cook for 5 minutes, then add the tomato purée and tamarind paste and stir again. Add the borlotti beans with their liquid, pour enough boiling water from a kettle over to generously cover the ingredients and stir. Cover the pan with a lid and cook for 45 minutes, stirring occasionally and checking the liquid level. Check and adjust the seasoning if desired before serving. This needs no accompaniment.

Traybakes

From all-in-one meals to superb side dishes and accompaniments – this is one of my favourite ways to cook food. It takes away the stress of multi-pan stove top cooking and lightens the load beautifully.

Aromatic Kofta & Potato Traybake

Traybakes are the answers to the prayers of a family cook. Chuck everything into a pan and cook it all together, then let everyone dive in without even removing it from its cooking vessel. I've kept this one simple with just meatballs and potatoes, as we know some people – kids especially – can be picky, but you can serve salad, vegetables or pulses on the side, if you wish.

SERVES 4–6

1 slice of bread, torn into pieces
6 tablespoons milk
500g (1lb 2oz) minced beef or lamb
1 large onion, very finely chopped
3 fat garlic cloves, minced
1 tablespoon garlic granules
1 tablespoon dried oregano
1 teaspoon ground turmeric
1 teaspoon ground cumin
1 teaspoon paprika
1 egg
1kg (2lb 4oz) potatoes, peeled and cut into discs just under 1cm (½ inch) thick

For the sauce
500g (1lb 2oz) passata
1 tablespoon garlic granules
2 teaspoons pul biber chilli flakes
1 teaspoon caster sugar
1 teaspoon paprika
2 tablespoons olive oil, plus an extra 2–3 tablespoons for drizzling
Maldon sea salt flakes and freshly ground black pepper

Preheat the oven to 200°C, 180°C fan (400°F), Gas Mark 6.

Mix all the sauce ingredients together in a bowl with a generous amount of salt and pepper. Set aside.

Soak the bread in the milk for few minutes until it absorbs all the liquid.

Put the soaked bread and all the remaining ingredients, except the potatoes, and a very generous amount of salt and pepper into a large rectangular ovenproof dish. Using your hands, work the ingredients together really well for several minutes until the mixture is soft and the bread has dissolved and is evenly dispersed along with the spices, onion and garlic.

Divide the mixture into about 26 equal portions and roll into balls. Arrange them in the dish, then add the potatoes among them. Carefully spoon over the sauce to ensure it mostly covers everything, drizzle with the extra olive oil, then bake for 30 minutes.

Remove from the oven and carefully stir the sauce over the potatoes and meatballs, then bake for another 30 minutes before serving.

GOES WELL WITH
Sesame, Garlic & Tahini Spinach (see page 207) or Okra with Tomato & Garlic (see page 208).

Spiced Pork & Pepper Traybake

This is a wonderfully simple recipe that is not only delicious but can be served in many ways – with salad, rice or potatoes as well as with wraps as shown here. But most importantly, it's very quick to throw together, and if catering for fewer people, you can either halve the recipe or freeze half of the marinated meat and peppers for another time.

SERVES 4–6

800g–1kg (1lb 12oz–2lb 4oz) pork shoulder steaks, cut into strips 1cm (½ inch) wide
2 large red or yellow peppers, cored, deseeded and cut into strips 1cm (½ inch) wide

For the marinade
1 large onion
3 fat garlic cloves
2 tablespoons tomato purée
1 tablespoon paprika
1 teaspoon ground cumin
2 teaspoons caster sugar
juice of ½ fat lemon
2 tablespoons olive oil
Maldon sea salt flakes and freshly ground black pepper

To serve (optional)
tortilla wraps
crème fraîche
grated mature Cheddar cheese
fresh coriander

Preheat your oven to its highest setting (with fan if it has one). Line a large baking tray with baking paper.

Blitz the onion with the garlic in a small bullet blender or mini food processor until very finely minced and their juices have been released.

Place the pork and peppers on the lined tray. Add the blitzed onion and garlic along with all the remaining marinade ingredients and season with a generous amount of salt and pepper. Using your hands, mix well to coat the pork and peppers evenly with the marinade, then spread out into a single layer. Roast for 18 minutes until charred but tender.

Remove from the oven and serve.

GOES WELL WITH
Popcorn Aubergine (see page 36) or My-style Batata Harra (see page 164).

My Family Traybake

Sometimes you need something that can be thrown together quickly, that doesn't involve making a big mess or juggling pans, and uses store-cupboard ingredients to help make a little go a lot further and keep hungry bellies happy – this is just that dish. Chicken with rice, spice and beans makes a satisfying, flavourful comfort meal any day of the week. It can be prepared ahead and reheated, and you can add in extra veg if you wish, but for me and my family this ticks all the boxes as it comes.

SERVES 6

- **650g (1lb 7oz) boneless, skinless chicken thighs**
- **400g (14oz) basmati rice**
- **300g (10½oz) can sweetcorn, drained**
- **400g (14oz) can cannellini beans, drained**
- **400g (14oz) can black beans or kidney beans, drained**
- **1 bunch of spring onions, thinly sliced**
- **800ml (1⅓ pints) boiling water, plus 75ml (2½fl oz) extra**
- **2 chicken stock pots or cubes**
- **6 tablespoons (about 125g/4½oz) tomato purée**
- **2 tablespoons tomato ketchup**
- **1 heaped tablespoon garlic granules**
- **2 tablespoons medium curry powder**
- **1 heaped teaspoon ground turmeric**
- **2–3 tablespoons olive oil**
- **Maldon sea salt flakes and freshly ground black pepper**

Preheat the oven to 220°C, 200°C fan (425°F), Gas Mark 7.

Chop the chicken thighs into bite-sized pieces and place in a large ovenproof dish – I prefer to do this using kitchen scissors, so no chopping board is required and the chicken falls straight into the dish. Add the rice, sweetcorn, beans and spring onions to the dish.

Pour the 800ml (1⅓ pints) boiling water into a measuring jug and add the stock pots or cubes, tomato purée and ketchup along with the garlic granules, spices, olive oil and a very heavy seasoning of salt (you will need lots to season the volume of rice and beans here) and some pepper, then stir until dissolved.

Pour the stock mixture over the ingredients in the dish and stir well to ensure everything is evenly combined. Cover with foil and bake for 45 minutes.

Remove from the oven, lift off the foil (but reserve it) and add the remaining 75ml (2½fl oz) boiling water, then bake for a further 15 minutes, uncovered.

Remove from the oven, cover with the reserved foil and leave to sit for 10–15 minutes. Fluff with a fork before serving.

GOES WELL WITH

Feta & Herb Yogurt Dip (see page 35) or Green Beans with Tomato & Garlic (see page 204).

Mango, Lime & Chilli Chicken

I use this exact cooking method to make every kind of traybaked chicken you could imagine. But this is a blend of store-cupboard staples with the addition of fresh lime to really push the flavour. If you don't have mango chutney, you can use any old sweet chutney from your stores instead. This recipe proves yet again that the best dishes never need to take long to put together. Serve with wraps, rice or a nice salad.

SERVES 3–4

about 600g (1lb 5oz) boneless, skinless chicken thighs

For the marinade

3 garlic cloves, crushed

3 tablespoons sweet mango chutney

2 tablespoons Greek-style yogurt

1 heaped teaspoon sriracha, or any chilli sauce

1 teaspoon ground turmeric

1 teaspoon paprika

1 teaspoon olive oil

finely grated zest and juice of 1 unwaxed lime

Maldon sea salt flakes and freshly ground black pepper

Preheat the oven to 220°C, 200°C fan (425°F), Gas Mark 7. Line a baking tray with baking paper.

Spread the chicken thighs out into a single layer on the lined tray.

Mix all the marinade ingredients together in a small bowl along with a generous amount of salt and pepper until well combined. Pour over the chicken thighs and then, using your hands, mix to coat both sides really well with the marinade.

Bake the chicken for 40 minutes until burnished, cooked through and juicy, then serve.

GOES WELL WITH

Sticky-glazed Spring Onions with Sesame (see page 153) or Traybaked Ludicrously Good Latke (see page 171).

Chicken & Potato Traybake with Za'atar & Lemon

This is so simple and full of flavour despite only using two key seasoning ingredients to bring it together. It only needs some hungry folk to share it with.

SERVES 4–6

1kg (2lb 4oz) bone-in, skin-on chicken thighs (8 or 9)

1.5kg (3lb 5oz) potatoes, peeled and cut into slices 1cm (½ inch) thick

3 tablespoons za'atar

finely grated zest and juice of 1 fat unwaxed lemon

4 tablespoons olive oil

Maldon sea salt flakes and freshly ground black pepper

Preheat the oven to 200°C, 180°C fan (400°F), Gas Mark 6. Line a large baking tray with baking paper.

Place all the ingredients on the lined tray and season with a generous amount of salt and pepper. Using your hands, mix well to coat the chicken and potatoes evenly with the flavourings and oil. Arrange the thighs on top of the potatoes, then roast for 45–50 minutes until the chicken has browned and is cooked through and the skin is lovely and crispy, and the potatoes are burnished.

To serve, I like to toss the potatoes in the pan juices before transferring to plates. Place the chicken on top of the potatoes, and pour over any remaining juices.

GOES WELL WITH

Labneh with Garlic, Tomatoes & Mint (see page 43) or Green Beans with Tomato & Garlic (see page 204).

Sticky-glazed Spring Onions with Sesame

If the Spaniards can obsess about eating *calçots* (a cross between a leek and a spring onion), then I can happily allow myself to eat spring onions as a vegetable in their own right. If you know my books, you'll know I've shared a few different spring onion recipes before, and here is another one of my favourites which is great served with grilled meats or fish or in wraps with kebabs.

SERVES 3–4

- **2 bunches of fat spring onions (14–16), thoroughly washed and patted dry**
- **olive oil spray or olive oil**
- **1 tablespoon sesame seeds (I used a mixture of black and white)**

For the glaze

- **2 tablespoons apricot jam**
- **finely grated zest of 1 unwaxed lemon and juice of ½**
- **½ teaspoon of freshly ground black pepper**
- **Maldon sea salt flakes**

Preheat the oven to 240°C, 220°C fan (475°F), Gas Mark 9. Line a large baking tray with baking paper.

Mix the glaze ingredients together in a small bowl until evenly combined.

Place the spring onions on the lined tray, spray or drizzle them with olive oil and rub in to ensure each one is well coated. Roast for 7 minutes.

Remove from the oven and pour the glaze over the spring onions until well coated. Sprinkle over the sesame seeds (do not stir), then roast for another 6 minutes or so until the seeds are toasted – check after 3 minutes to ensure the spring onions are not drying out. Serve immediately.

GOES WELL WITH

Sweet & Spicy Spatchcocked Chicken (see page 176) or Sticky Roasted Salmon with Tamarind & Chilli (see page 190).

My-style Batata Harra

Literally meaning 'spicy potato', *batata harra* is a popular Lebanese potato dish that is full of flavour and the perfect side dish for so many things, though quite frankly I'm happy to eat it on its own with a couple of fried eggs on top. My version is merely inspired by the classic (which is usually fried) – here I roast the potatoes instead for ease and then give them a little toss in a zingy, spicy coating to serve. It is the perfect treatment for the humble spud and adds a new twist that everyone will love.

SERVES 4–6

750g (1lb 10oz) new potatoes, cut into about 1.5cm (⅝ inch) cubes
2 teaspoons ground turmeric
1 heaped teaspoon garlic granules
olive oil
Maldon sea salt flakes and freshly ground black pepper

For the spicy coating
1 small packet (about 30g/1oz) of fresh coriander, very finely chopped
1 teaspoon chilli flakes
finely grated zest and juice of 1 fat unwaxed lime
2 tablespoons olive oil
1 teaspoon caster sugar

Preheat the oven to 200°C, 180°C fan (400°F), Gas Mark 6. Line your largest baking tray with baking paper.

Place the potatoes on the lined tray, add the turmeric and garlic granules and season with a generous amount of salt and pepper. Drizzle with the olive oil and then, using your hands, mix well to coat the potatoes evenly with the flavourings and oil. Spread the potatoes out into a single layer and roast for 45 minutes.

Meanwhile, mix your spicy coating ingredients together in a small bowl, season well with salt and pepper and mix again, then set aside.

Remove the potatoes from the oven, pour the spicy coating over them in the tray and mix well. Leave them to stand and absorb the flavours for a couple of minutes before serving.

GOES WELL WITH
Ćevapčići (see page 88), Shami Koftas (see page 121) or Marinated Steak Strips with Tamato Sauce & Garlic Yogurt (see page 180).

Firecracker Cauliflower Pilaf Traybake

I love cauliflower but hate boiling it because you lose all the goodness and flavour, and yet I find steaming it a bit of a faff. So, this lovely little recipe is perfect for capturing its natural flavour but it's also an easy 'throw-it-all-together' bake. You can add any veggies you may have lying around too, but I like to keep it simple and just used the stalk, leaves and florets of the cauliflower itself which are all equally edible and delicious.

SERVES 4 – 6

1 cauliflower with leaves, sliced into discs 2.5cm (1 inch) thick and then broken up into small florets, stalk thinly sliced and leaves roughly chopped

300g (10½oz) basmati rice

4 fat garlic cloves, crushed

1 tablespoon ginger purée/paste or 10cm (4 inch) piece of fresh root ginger, peeled and finely grated

1 level teaspoon chilli flakes

2 teaspoons ground turmeric

2 teaspoons paprika

50g (1¾oz) desiccated coconut

olive oil

1 vegetable stock pot or cube

50g (1¾oz) butter or plant-based alternative

700ml (1¼ pints) boiling water

Maldon sea salt flakes and freshly ground black pepper

To serve (optional)

Greek yogurt

lemon wedges

Preheat the oven to 200°C, 180°C fan (400°F), Gas Mark 6.

Put the cauliflower, rice, garlic, ginger, spices and coconut into a large ovenproof dish, then drizzle with olive oil and season with a very generous amount of salt and pepper (especially salt). Using your hands, mix well to coat the cauliflower and rice evenly with the flavourings and oil.

Add the stock pot or cube to a measuring jug with the butter or butter alternative, pour over the boiling water and stir until they have dissolved/melted. Pour the stock mixture over the ingredients in the dish and cover tightly with foil. Bake for 50 minutes–1 hour, removing the foil after 30 minutes to carefully mix the ingredients together and then replacing it, until the rice is cooked. Once done, remove from the oven, lift off the foil and stir carefully using a fork, then serve with yogurt and lemon wedges.

GOES WELL WITH

Feta & Herb Yogurt Dip (see page 35) or Green Beans with Tomato & Garlic (see page 204).

The Really Useful Vegetable Traybake

'How do I love thee? Let me count the ways.' These are the words of poet Elizabeth Barrett Browning, which are very apt for this recipe because it is so versatile and useful that you can make countless versions. You can eat it on its own, as an accompaniment to roasts or add it to rice and pasta dishes, salads, stews and so much more. It's literally a godsend in a tray – easy, no frying and everything cooks at the same time!

SERVES 6

2 large red onions, halved and cut into 8mm (⅜ inch) thick half moons

1 large aubergine, cut into about 1cm (½ inch) cubes

1 large red pepper, cored, deseeded and cut into 1.5cm (⅝ inch) cubes

1 large courgette, quartered, then cut into 1.5cm (⅝ inch) cubes

1 teaspoon cumin seeds

1 heaped teaspoon paprika

1 teaspoon garlic granules

1 teaspoon dried oregano

olive oil

Maldon sea salt flakes and freshly ground black pepper

Preheat the oven to 200°C, 180°C fan (400°F), Gas Mark 6. Line a large baking tray with baking paper.

Place all your prepared vegetables on the lined tray, add the spices, garlic granules, oregano and a heavy seasoning of salt and pepper and drizzle very generously with olive oil. Using your hands, mix well to coat all the vegetables evenly with the flavourings and oil.

Spread the vegetables out into a single layer and roast for 35–40 minutes until nicely browned. Remove from the oven and serve, or leave to cool and use as part of another dish.

GOES WELL WITH

Add to any Three Ways with Pasta Sauce (see pages 17–19) or Shami Koftas (see page 121).

Roasted Aubergine with Harissa Tomato Sauce & Mozzarella

You'd be forgiven for thinking this is a kind of aubergine *parmigiana*, as it's very similar, but by rights I can't call it that because I haven't used any Parmesan. This is very much my own twist on that classic recipe with a spicy kick and, more importantly, it's so easy and mess-free to make.

SERVES 4

- **2 large aubergines, cut in half lengthways with the stalks left on**
- **olive oil**
- **400g (14oz) can best-quality chopped tomatoes (I use Mutti)**
- **2 tablespoons rose harissa**
- **1 tablespoon runny honey**
- **1 teaspoon garlic granules**
- **4 large basil leaves**
- **200g (7oz) ball of cows' milk mozzarella, drained**
- **Maldon sea salt flakes and freshly ground black pepper**

Preheat the oven to 200°C, 180°C fan (400°F), Gas Mark 6. Line a large baking tray with baking paper.

Place the 4 aubergine halves cut-side up on the tray. Brush them generously with olive oil, then roast for 30 minutes.

Meanwhile, mix the canned tomatoes, harissa, honey and garlic granules together in a bowl with a generous amount of salt and pepper.

Remove the aubergines from oven and then, using a small knife, carefully make long cuts through the flesh but without cutting through the skin. Divide the tomato mixture on top of the aubergine halves and place a large basil leaf in the centre of each.

Cut the mozzarella into quarters, then cut each quarter into 3. Place 3 pieces on each aubergine, then bake for 15 minutes until the mozzarella has melted. Remove from the oven and serve.

GOES WELL WITH

Garlic & Potato Dip (see page 28), Tangy Ottoman Orzo Salad (see page 64) or Pomegranate Sweet Potatoes (see page 168).

Roasted Spiced Aubergine & Tomato with Yogurt & Herbs

I can never get enough of the combination of aubergines with silky smooth yogurt, and this is a great dish for a mezze-style vibe – ideal for sharing and quick to put together.

SERVES 4–6

- **1 large aubergine, cut into discs just over 1cm (½ inch) thick and then cut into 1cm (½ inch) cubes**
- **½ teaspoon paprika**
- **½ teaspoon ground cumin**
- **1 teaspoon dried mint**
- **olive oil**
- **2 large tomatoes, halved and each half cut into 6 pieces**
- **500g (1lb 2oz) thick Greek yogurt**
- **1 fat garlic clove, crushed**
- **handful of mint leaves and fresh coriander, finely chopped**
- **½ teaspoon pul biber chilli fakes**
- **Maldon sea salt flakes and freshly ground black pepper**

Preheat the oven to 200°C, 180°C fan (400°F), Gas Mark 6. Line a large baking tray with baking paper.

Place the aubergine on the lined tray and sprinkle over the paprika, cumin, ½ teaspoon of the dried mint and a heavy seasoning of salt and pepper, then drizzle generously with olive oil and use your hands to coat the aubergine cubes in the seasonings. Spread out the aubergine so that it occupies half the tray, then spread out the tomatoes on the other side. Season the tomatoes with pepper only (no salt), drizzle with olive oil and sprinkle with the remaining ½ teaspoon dried mint.

Roast the aubergine and tomatoes for 35 minutes or until soft and browned. Remove from the oven and leave to cool until warm.

Mix the yogurt with the garlic and a generous amount of salt and pepper in a bowl, then spread on to a platter. Season the warm roasted veg with salt and stir carefully, then arrange the veg on top of the yogurt. Sprinkle over the chopped herbs and pul biber and add a little extra olive oil before serving.

GOES WELL WITH

Feta, Tarragon & Spice Rolls (see page 31) or Ćevapčići (see page 88).

VEGETARIAN

Halloumi, Pepper & Spring Onion Tart

I've often made quiches using puff pastry instead of shortcrust – puff pastry just feels so much lighter, and I really love its crunch when freshly baked. If you want your quiche filling to be a little deeper than mine, simply use a slightly smaller dish, but my version will feed a few more people.

SERVES 6

- **plain flour, for dusting**
- **500g (1lb 2oz) block of puff pastry**
- **3 large eggs**
- **300ml (10fl oz) double cream**
- **125g (4½oz) halloumi cheese, grated**
- **75g (2¾oz) pitted Kalamata olives, halved**
- **4 large spring onions, thinly sliced**
- **2 large roasted red peppers in brine (from a jar), drained and diced**
- **½ small packet (about 15g/½oz) of dill, finely chopped**
- **Maldon sea salt flakes and freshly ground black pepper**

Preheat the oven to 200°C, 180°C fan (400°F), Gas Mark 6.

Dust a clean work surface with a little flour and roll the pastry out into a rectangle large enough to cover the base and sides of a rectangular ovenproof dish about 32 x 20cm/12¾ x 8 inches. Ensure the pastry fits snugly into all the corners of the dish and up the sides.

Place the eggs and cream in a large mixing bowl and lightly whisk using a fork, then season with salt and a very generous amount of pepper. Add all the remaining ingredients, except the milk, and mix until well combined. Pour the mixture into the pastry base in the dish, then bake for 40 minutes.

Once the filling has cooked and is set, remove from the oven and leave to cool slightly before serving.

GOES WELL WITH

Carrot, Orange & Pepper Salad (see page 67) or Roasted Spice Aubergines & Tomato with Yogurt & Herbs (see page 162).

Aubergine & Sweet Potato Kari

This is a genius traybaked curry recipe because it avoids having to fry aubergines, which can be a messy process and consume lots of oil, but also because the aubergines and sweet potato conveniently cook at the same time. The sauce is nutty, creamy, comforting – and vegan! My husband is a diehard meat eater and doesn't always appreciate aubergines, but he loves this, so you have to try it for yourself. Try stirring in some fresh spinach leaves or frozen peas when you add in the sauce – it's such a versatile and delicious dish, and good served with flatbreads or rice.

SERVES 4

2 large aubergines, cut into about 2.5cm (1 inch) chunks

500g (1lb 2oz) sweet potatoes, peeled and cut into about 2.5cm (1 inch) chunks

olive oil

handful of chopped fresh coriander, to serve

For the sauce

250ml (9fl oz) coconut cream

2 heaped tablespoons peanut butter (I use crunchy)

2 tablespoons rose harissa

1 tablespoon tamarind paste

Maldon sea salt flakes and freshly ground black pepper

Mix the sauce ingredients together in a bowl, seasoning well with salt and pepper.

Preheat the oven to 200°C, 180°C fan (400°F), Gas Mark 6. Line your largest baking tray with baking paper.

Place the aubergines and sweet potatoes on the lined tray, drizzle with olive oil and then, using your hands, mix well to coat them evenly with the oil. Spread out into a single layer, season well with salt and pepper and roast for 30 minutes.

Remove from the oven, pour the sauce over the vegetables and carefully stir to coat them, then bake for a final 5 minutes. Remove from the oven and sprinkle with the coriander before serving.

GOES WELL WITH

Lemon & Black Pepper Cabbage (see page 197) or Green Beans with Tomato & Garlic (see page 204).

Pomegranate Sweet Potatoes

I never tire of eating sweet potatoes. I can never understand when people say they don't really like them, because even if you're not a big fan of sweet things there is always a spice or an ingredient that marries well with them to balance out their natural sweetness beautifully. This recipe is the perfect example of a sweet potato pairing with a simple marinade, resulting in absolute bliss.

SERVES 3–4

500g (1lb 2oz) sweet potatoes, peeled

1 tablespoon pomegranate molasses

1 teaspoon garlic granules

olive oil

Maldon sea salt flakes and freshly ground black pepper

Preheat the oven to 200°C, 180°C fan (400°F), Gas Mark 6. Line a large baking tray with baking paper.

Cut the sweet potatoes into half moons, 1cm (½ inch) thick, and place on the lined tray. Add the pomegranate molasses and garlic granules along with a little drizzle of olive oil and a good amount of salt and pepper then, using your hands, mix well until each piece of sweet potato is evenly coated with the flavourings and oil.

Spread the sweet potato pieces out into a single layer, then bake for 25–30 minutes until cooked and the glaze is chewy and brown on outside. Serve immediately.

GOES WELL WITH

Sweet & Spicy Spatchcocked Chicken (see page 176) or Marinated Steak Strips with Tomato Sauce & Garlic Yogurt (see page 180).

Traybaked Ludicrously Good Latke

I love hash browns, röstis and latkes – give me crispy fried potatoes of any description and I'm a happy girl. But I won't lie and tell you that I love frying, because the truth is, if I can avoid it, I do – it's messy, greasy, smelly and uses quite a bit of oil, which is pretty costly, so I save my frying for only when absolutely essential. But how to produce a perfectly crispy latke by baking? Well, I've managed to do it, and I'm really happy with the results and I know you will be, too.

SERVES 3–4

1–1.5kg (2lb 4oz–3lb 5oz) potatoes, peeled or unpeeled and scrubbed, coarsely grated
1 very large onion, grated or blitzed in a small bullet blender or mini food processor
1 heaped teaspoon dried sage
1 heaped teaspoon dried oregano
1 heaped teaspoon garlic granules
2 tablespoons cornflour
olive oil spray or olive oil
Maldon sea salt flakes and freshly ground black pepper

Preheat the oven to 200°C, 180°C fan (400°F), Gas Mark 6. Line a large baking tray with baking paper.

Put the grated potatoes and onion into a large mixing bowl with a generous amount of salt and then, using your hands, mix together well. Leave to sit for 10 minutes.

Place the potato mixture in a clean cotton tea towel, gather the edges and spend a good 5 minutes squeezing out as much liquid as you can – the drier the mixture is, the crispier it will be. Transfer the mixture to a dry bowl, season again with more salt and pepper, and add the dried herbs, garlic granules and cornflour, then mix really well until evenly combined.

Spray or brush the baking paper with a generous amount of olive oil and loosely scatter the potato mixture evenly on it – I like to make one big rectangular latke, but you can form it into any shape you like, or even small individual latkes. Pat the latke flat without pressing too hard, tidy the edges if needed, then spray or brush the top generously all over with olive oil.

Bake for 40–45 minutes until deeply crisp and golden with burnished edges. If making smaller ones, you will need to check them after baking for 35 minutes or so. Remove from the oven, cut into squares and serve.

GOES WELL WITH

Spicy Orange Chicken Bites (see page 95), Mango, Lime & Chilli Chicken (see page 146) or Sweet & Spicy Spatchcocked Chicken (see page 176).

Baked Sweet Potatoes with Yogurt, Harissa & Chives

Think of a classic baked potato, but Eastern style! The wonderfully sweet nature of these potatoes not only stands up to the heat of harissa but is perfectly balanced by the tangy yogurt, and the chives finish things beautifully. Midweek comfort galore!

SERVES 2–4

- **2 sweet potatoes, about 250g (9oz) each, unpeeled and scrubbed**
- **4 tablespoons thick Greek yogurt**
- **2 teaspoons rose harissa**
- **⅓ small packet (generous 5g/¼oz) of chives, very finely chopped**
- **Maldon sea salt flakes and freshly ground black pepper**
- **1 lime, cut into 4 wedges, to serve (optional)**

Preheat the oven to 220°C, 200°C fan (425°F), Gas Mark 7. Line a baking tray with baking paper.

Place the sweet potatoes on the lined tray and bake for 45 minutes until the flesh inside is soft.

Remove from the oven, split the sweet potatoes in half and sit flesh-side up. Season well with salt and pepper, then add 1 tablespoon Greek yogurt to each half, top with ½ teaspoon harissa and finish with the chives. Serve with the lime wedges for squeezing over if desired.

GOES WELL WITH

Ćevapčići (see page 88), Juicy Joojeh Koobideh (see page 92) or Marinated Steak Strips with Tamato Sauce & Garlic Yogurt (see page 180).

Something Special

These are my go-to recipes for when I want something with a bit of pizzazz, or an ultimate comfort dish no matter what the occasion – perfect for a special menu for sharing.

Sweet & Spicy Spatchcocked Chicken

I'm a huge fan of cooking chicken spatchcock-style because the method allows you the ultimate convenience of roasting a whole chicken in half the time it would otherwise take and ensures a lovely, juicy bird every time. You can leave it to marinate in the fridge overnight if you like, but it's also fine to roast straight away.

SERVES 4–6

1.5kg (3lb 5oz) whole chicken

For the marinade
2 tablespoons runny honey
1 tablespoon tamarind paste
1 tablespoon rose harissa
1 teaspoon olive oil
1 teaspoon paprika
1 teaspoon garlic granules
½ teaspoon ground cinnamon
Maldon sea salt flakes and freshly ground black pepper

Preheat the oven to 220°C, 200°C fan (425°F), Gas Mark 7. Line a large baking tray with baking paper.

To spatchcock the chicken, place it breast-side down on a chopping board. Using a pair of poultry shears or heavy-duty scissors, cut down either side of the backbone and then remove the bone. Turn the chicken over breast-side up and gently press down on it with both hands until as flat as possible. Transfer the spatchcocked bird to the lined tray.

Mix all the marinade ingredients in a small bowl along with some salt and pepper. Rub the marinade all over the chicken, then roast for 45 minutes until well browned and cooked through – the juices should run clear when the thickest part of the thigh is pierced with the tip of a sharp knife.

Remove from the oven, cover loosely with foil and leave to rest for 10 minutes or so before serving.

GOES WELL WITH

Three Ways with Rice (see pages 20–3), Pomegranate Sweet Potatoes (see page 168), Green Beans with Tomato & Garlic (see page 204) or Okra with Tomato & Garlic (see page 208).

Murgh Karahi

Inspired by my love of Pakistani-style curries, which are so different to Indian ones, this is such a lovely, fragrant example and has quickly become one of my most-cooked curries at home. You can halve the quantities if you like, but I strongly recommend you make the whole recipe and freeze a batch for another day – you'll thank me for it! Serve with naan or basmati rice.

SERVES 6

vegetable oil

2 large onions, halved and thinly sliced into half moons

1kg (2lb 4oz) boneless, skinless chicken thighs, each cut into 3–4 bite-sized pieces

4 large garlic cloves, minced

10cm (4 inch) piece of fresh root ginger, peeled and grated, or 2 tablespoons ginger purée/paste

3 green rocket chillies, finely chopped

1 tablespoon ground turmeric

1 heaped teaspoon ground cumin

1 heaped teaspoon ground coriander

½ teaspoon ground cinnamon

400g (14oz) can chopped tomatoes

generous handful of chopped fresh coriander

Maldon sea salt flakes and freshly ground black pepper

Place a large saucepan over a medium-high heat, pour in enough vegetable oil to coat the base and cook the onions until softened and translucent. Add the chicken, garlic, ginger, chillies and spices and season with salt and a very generous amount of pepper. Stir well until the chicken is coated in all the spices and cook for 5 minutes.

Pour in the canned tomatoes and just enough boiling water from a kettle to barely cover the chicken. Stir really well and then cover the pan with a lid and cook over a gentle medium heat for 1 hour, stirring occasionally to prevent burning but ensuring there is a nice bubbling coming from the pan.

Remove the lid and cook, uncovered, for a final 30 minutes – increase the heat slightly to reduce the liquid if necessary – then check and adjust the seasoning. Stir through the coriander at the last minute and then serve.

GOES WELL WITH

Feta & Herb Yogurt Dip (see page 35) or Carrot, Orange & Pepper Salad (see page 67).

Marinated Steak Strips with Tomato Sauce & Garlic Yogurt

Iskender kebap **is one of my favourite Turkish dishes, named after Alexander (Iskender) the Great. It consists of strips of thinly sliced lamb on a bed of bread, topped with a simple tomato sauce, some grilled tomatoes and Turkish peppers and finished with foaming melted butter. This recipe is wholly inspired by my love of that dish, but I've made it much easier so that you can throw it together in very little time.**

SERVES 2–3

2 beef steaks of your choice (such as sirloin, rump, fillet, ribeye or bavette), 200–250g (7–9oz) each

Maldon sea salt flakes and freshly ground black pepper

For the tomato sauce

olive oil

1 tablespoon tomato purée

½ teaspoon paprika

½ teaspoon pul biber chilli flakes

2–3 large tomatoes, coarsely grated into a bowl

25g (1oz) butter

For the meat marinade

1 teaspoon dried oregano

1 teaspoon garlic granules

1 teaspoon paprika

½ teaspoon pul biber chilli flakes

To serve

150g (5½oz) Greek-style yogurt

1 small garlic clove, minced

1 large tortilla wrap

handful of chopped flat leaf parsley

Mix the yogurt, garlic and some salt and pepper together in a small bowl and set aside until ready to serve.

For the sauce, place a heavy-based frying pan over a medium heat, drizzle in some olive oil and add the tomato purée, spices and a generous amount of salt. Stir and cook for 6–8 minutes until the oil bleeds out orange/red from the paste mixture. Add the grated tomatoes and cook for 8–10 minutes, stirring all the time to prevent burning. Decant into the bowl you used for grating the tomatoes and set aside.

Cut the beef into wafer-thin strips as best you can and place in a separate bowl. Add all the marinade ingredients, drizzle with 2–3 tablespoons of olive oil, then, using your hands, mix well to coat the meat in the marinade. Leave to marinate at room temperature for 10 minutes.

Wipe the pan and place over a high heat. Once it begins to smoke, pour in a generous amount of olive oil, then add the beef – spread it out immediately into a single layer – it will only need a few minutes of cooking time, so be quick. Season well with salt and stir-fry, until the meat is charred and cooked through but not overcooked. Remove from the pan to a warmed plate and leave to rest covered with foil.

Add the butter and tomato sauce to the pan over a medium-high heat and stir until the butter has melted into the sauce.

To serve, lay the tortilla wrap on a large plate, add the beef, then pour over the tomato sauce. Dot with the garlic yogurt and finish with the parsley.

GOES WELL WITH

Three Ways with Rice (see pages 20–3), Pomegranate Sweet Potatoes (see page 168) or Green Beans with Tomato & Garlic (see page 204).

Nihari-style Lamb Shanks

This is by no means an authentic recipe, because the real version is painstakingly laborious and involves a lot of processes and ingredients, so it just isn't something I'd make too often at home. Enter my one-pan-homage to this incredibly special recipe, in which I've skipped lots of vital stages in favour of simplicity, but it's equally enjoyable, and pretty unbeatable for a one-pot wonder. Serve with rice or potatoes.

SERVES 4

ghee or vegetable oil
2 large onions, halved and very finely sliced into half moons
6 green cardamom pods, lightly cracked or bashed
6 black peppercorns
1 teaspoon fennel seeds
2 teaspoons ground cumin
2 teaspoons ground coriander
1 heaped teaspoon chilli powder
1 teaspoon ground cinnamon
1 teaspoon ground turmeric
½ teaspoon ground cloves
½ teaspoon ground nutmeg
6 fat garlic cloves, finely chopped
1 tablespoon ginger purée/paste or 2.5cm (1 inch) piece of fresh root ginger, peeled and grated
3 whole green chillies, stalks removed
2 tablespoons desiccated coconut
4 tablespoons Greek-style yogurt
juice of ½ lemon
4 lamb shanks
Maldon sea salt flakes and freshly ground black pepper

To serve

2–3 large handfuls of shop-bought crispy fried onions
handful of fresh coriander, roughly chopped

Place a large saucepan over a high heat and pour in enough ghee or vegetable oil to generously coat the base. Once hot, add the onions and fry for 8–10 minutes until nicely browned with crispy edges, stirring occasionally.

Reduce the heat to medium, then add all the dry spices and the garlic, stir well and cook for a couple of minutes. Stir in the ginger, chillies, coconut, yogurt and lemon juice until well combined, then lay the lamb shanks in the pan, season generously with salt and pepper and mix to coat them evenly with the other ingredients. Pour over enough boiling water from a kettle to barely cover the shanks, cover the pan with a lid and cook for 2–2½ hours or until the meat is tender, turning the shanks a couple of times and checking they are immersed in liquid.

Remove the lid and taste – adjust the seasoning if desired, then serve with the crispy fried onions and coriander on top to finish.

GOES WELL WITH

Firecracker Cauliflower Pilaf Traybake (see page 157) or My-style Batata Harra (see page 154).

Afghani Qorma Kofta

Ever since I was a kid, I've had a real love for Afghani food – it made me want to get to know the cuisine, and having learned more about it I've realized that it's quite similar to Persian. This *qorma* (meaning 'stew') kofta is homely, deeply delicious and perfect with flatbreads or rice.

SERVES 4

2 onions
vegetable oil
2 green rocket chillies
4 fat garlic cloves, crushed
2 teaspoons ground coriander
1 teaspoon ground cumin
½ teaspoon ground turmeric
½ teaspoon freshly ground black pepper
2 tablespoons tomato purée
2 large tomatoes, finely chopped
400ml (14fl oz) boiling water

For the koftas
500g (1lb 2oz) minced lamb or beef (20% fat)
1 heaped teaspoon ground cumin
1 heaped teaspoon ground coriander
1 teaspoon ground turmeric
½ teaspoon hot chilli powder
½ teaspoon ground cinnamon
½ teaspoon freshly ground black pepper
1 small packet (about 30g/1oz) of fresh coriander, finely chopped, half reserved for garnish
Maldon sea salt flakes

Blitz the onions in a small bullet blender or mini food processor until finely minced and their juices have been released. Strain off the juices through a sieve set over a small bowl and reserve.

For the sauce, place a large saucepan over a medium-high heat and drizzle in enough vegetable oil to coat the base. Add half the minced onions and cook for 8–10 minutes until they start to brown around the edges.

Pull the stalks off the chillies (don't cut them out, as you don't want to break the chilli) and add them whole with the garlic. Cook for a couple of minutes, then add the spices and tomato purée, stir well and cook for 3–4 minutes.

Stir in the tomatoes and the reserved onion juices, reduce the heat to medium, then simmer, stirring occasionally, while you make the koftas.

Put the remaining minced onions along with all the kofta ingredients and some salt into a mixing bowl and, using your hands, work the ingredients together really well for a few minutes until you have a smooth and evenly combined paste. Divide the mixture into about 18–20 equal portions and roll into balls, then gently press and flatten into round patties roughly 6cm (2½ inch) in diameter.

Pour the boiling water into the tomato sauce mixture in the pan and stir well, then carefully add the koftas, without stirring – until they are cooked they will remain soft and may easily crumble. To ensure they are immersed, shake the pan gently and they should sink into the sauce. Cover the pan with a lid and cook the koftas for 20 minutes.

Remove the lid, gently stir and cook for another 15 minutes, uncovered, to reduce the sauce (you can increase the heat a little if it seems too watery). Once you have achieved the desired sauce consistency, check and adjust the seasoning, adding more salt and pepper if needed, then serve topped with the reserved coriander.

GOES WELL WITH
Okra with Tomato & Garlic (see page 208).

Shuwa-style Lamb Shoulder

I don't think I ever tire of roasted lamb recipes, and this one is a much-simplified version of a wonderful Omani dish where the lamb is buried underground and cooked very slowly until it falls apart. The marinade is earthy, tangy and spicy, and I don't mind telling you that I ate quite a bit of it when I first made this. Lamb shoulder, for me, is the perfect cut to use, as it never fails to be less than wonderfully tender.

SERVES 6

1.8–2kg (4–4lb 8oz) lamb shoulder on the bone

For the marinade

1 small onion

6 garlic cloves, minced

1 tablespoon ginger purée/paste

2 tablespoons tamarind paste

seeds from 6 green cardamom pods, ground using a pestle and mortar

2 teaspoons ground cumin

2 teaspoons ground coriander

1 heaped teaspoon dried lime powder (or a good squeeze of lemon juice)

1 teaspoon ground turmeric

1 teaspoon ground cinnamon

½–1 teaspoon chilli flakes

½ teaspoon ground cloves

½ teaspoon freshly ground black pepper

generous amount of Maldon sea salt flakes

Preheat the oven to 180°C, 160°C fan (350°F), Gas Mark 4. Line a large baking tray with baking paper.

Cut 3 slashes 1cm (½ inch) deep into the lamb shoulder and place fat-side up on the lined tray.

Blitz the onion, garlic and ginger purée/paste together in a small bullet blender or mini food processor until you have a very smooth paste. Decant into a bowl. Add the remaining marinade ingredients and mix together until evenly combined.

Pour the marinade over the lamb and rub it in all over, especially into the cuts and on the fat side. Cover the tray tightly with foil (try to dome the foil a little to avoid it touching the marinade) and roast for 5 hours. Remove from the oven and serve.

GOES WELL WITH

Chickpea, Garlic, Cinnamon & Cumin Rice (see page 22), Spiced Pear & Feta Salad with Watercress, Chicory & Pomegranate (see page 58) or Pomegranate Sweet Potatoes (see page 172).

Sticky Roasted Salmon with Tamarind & Chilli

I love the fact that salmon has such an enormous capacity to stand up to big, bold flavours, which makes it the perfect choice of fish when dealing with spice. Roasted salmon of every description is a house staple of mine, the spicier and stickier the better, and this is a new favourite. Be sure to use the regular brown tamarind paste rather than the really dark kind which will require more sweetening.

SERVES 3–4

600g (1lb 5oz) piece of salmon fillet (middle, not tail end), at room temperature

For the marinade

2 tablespoons runny honey

1 tablespoon tamarind paste

1 heaped teaspoon garlic granules

1 teaspoon chilli flakes

Maldon sea salt flakes and freshly ground black pepper

Preheat the oven to 220°C, 200°C fan (425°F), Gas Mark 7. Line a baking tray with baking paper.

Mix the marinade ingredients together with a generous amount of salt and pepper in a small bowl until well combined.

Place the salmon skin-side down on the lined tray and coat the top and sides evenly with the marinade. Alternatively, you can cut the salmon into 3 or 4 individual portions and coat with the marinade in the same way.

Roast for 20–22 minutes for a whole piece or 16–18 minutes for individual pieces. Serve immediately.

GOES WELL WITH

Apple, Lentil, Ginger & Cranberry Rice Salad (see page 71) or Pomegranate Sweet Potatoes (see page 172).

Vegetables & Sides

Because we are often guilty of not eating enough vegetables, take some 'veg-spiration' from the recipes in this chapter! For side dishes that sing, there is something here for every occasion.

Braised Leeks with Lemon & Garlic

While I adore leeks, I never eat enough of them (aside from the occasional soup or pie filling), which is a shame. This pure celebration of leeks is a popular Syrian dish called *barasya*, in which you simply braise the leeks in olive oil and add your flavourings. The end result is versatile enough to be served as a side to many things such as roasted or grilled poultry or fish, but I like it with good bread and a little Greek yogurt.

SERVES 3–4

3 large leeks (about 500g/1lb 2oz total weight), trimmed, cleaned and cut into 2.5cm (1 inch) thick pieces
olive oil
3 garlic cloves, minced
1 teaspoon garlic granules
juice of ½ lemon
Maldon sea salt flakes and freshly ground black pepper
generous handful of fresh coriander, roughly chopped, to serve

Put the leek pieces into a heatproof bowl or saucepan, pour over boiling water to cover and leave to soak for 30 minutes, then drain. This will soften them a little and rinse out any trapped dirt between the layers of the leeks.

Place a frying pan over a medium heat, pour in enough olive oil to more than generously coat the base and add the leeks. They will sizzle, as they still contain water, but don't worry because it's great for cooking them. Cover the pan with a lid and braise the leeks for 15 minutes, shaking the pan occasionally to ensure they don't burn.

Remove the lid – the leeks should have softened slightly – stir and break them down to encourage the rings to come apart, then add the fresh garlic and garlic granules and a good amount of salt and pepper and mix well before squeezing over the lemon juice. Stir again, replace the lid and cook for another 5 minutes. Remove the lid, stir and increase the heat for a final couple of minutes, stirring occasionally. Check the seasoning, sprinkle with the coriander, then serve.

GOES WELL WITH

Firecracker Cauliflower Pilaf Traybake (see page 153) or Sticky Roasted Salmon with Tamarind & Chilli (see page 190).

Lemon & Black Pepper Cabbage

I do love cabbage and I'm always finding new and interesting ways to serve it to the family. I've borrowed some of the ingredients from hummus for this recipe, plus a heavy milling of black pepper – the combination really works.

SERVES 3–4

1 teaspoon tahini
2 garlic cloves, crushed
juice of ½ fat lemon
¾ teaspoon coarsely ground black pepper
olive oil
500g (1lb 2oz) white cabbage, very thinly sliced
2 pinches of pul biber chilli flakes
Maldon sea salt flakes
toasted sesame seeds (a mix of black and white), to serve (optional)

Mix together the tahini, garlic, lemon juice, pepper, a generous amount of salt and 2 tablespoons of warm water in a small bowl until evenly combined. Set aside.

Place a large pan over a medium heat and drizzle in a generous amount of olive oil. Add the cabbage and stir to coat in the oil, then cover the pan with a lid and cook for 8–10 minutes. Remove the lid and stir, then replace the lid and cook for another 5 minutes or until the cabbage has softened to your liking (I like to retain a little bite).

Remove the lid, add the tahini mixture and stir well to mix. Add about 2 tablespoons or so of warm water to slacken the sauce so that it coats the cabbage. Check and adjust the seasoning, then sprinkle with the pul biber and serve topped with some toasted sesame seeds, if using.

GOES WELL WITH

Mango, Lime & Chilli Chicken (see page 144) or Aubergine & Sweet Potato Kari (see page 168).

Creamy Butter Beans with Lemon & Tahini

This is a great store-cupboard recipe that comes together quickly and easily. It's creamy, comforting and really delicious. I used butter beans, but you can make the recipe with any canned beans you like. Serve it on top of some buttered toast or alongside other dishes.

SERVES 2–3

olive oil
4 fat garlic cloves, thinly sliced
1 teaspoon dried oregano
½ teaspoon pul biber chilli flakes
1 tablespoon tahini
400g (14oz) can butter beans, including the liquid from the can
juice of ½ fat lemon
Maldon sea salt flakes and freshly ground black pepper
toasted bread, to serve

Place a small saucepan over a medium heat and drizzle in enough olive oil to coat the base. Once hot, fry the garlic until it begins to turn golden around the edges. Stir in the oregano and pul biber, then add the tahini and stir well until dissolved.

Add the beans with their liquid along with the lemon juice. Season everything well with salt and pepper and stir again, then increase the heat to medium-high and cook for 8–10 minutes, stirring occasionally, until the liquid in the pan has reduced. Once the mixture is nice and thick, serve on buttered toast.

GOES WELL WITH

Feta & Herb Yogurt Dip (see page 35) or Green Beans with Tomato & Garlic (see page 204).

Charred Corn & Vegetables in a Coconut Curry Sauce

If I'm going to eat a veg-only meal, I want it to be an explosion of flavour, but moreover I want it to satisfy me in the same way any other meal would. This is a really great way to eat a colourful and delicious array of vegetables in a comforting, pleasing curry-like sauce. The charring of the corn gives it a lovely subtle smoky flavour that adds so much to the dish. This is perfect on its own, or try serving it with rice, noodles or topped with a soft-boiled egg.

SERVES 4

2 sweetcorn cobs, husked if necessary and kernels sliced off with a knife
olive oil
6 garlic cloves, finely chopped
1 onion, finely chopped
200g (7oz) fine green beans, trimmed and halved
200g (7oz) Tenderstem broccoli, chopped into small bite-sized pieces (you can also use cauliflower florets)
1 tablespoon rose harissa
1 tablespoon medium or mild curry powder
250ml (9fl oz) coconut cream
juice of ½ lime
Maldon sea salt flakes and freshly ground black pepper

Heat a large, deep dry frying pan or a saucepan, which has a lid, over a high heat, add the sweetcorn kernels and leave to char for a good 6–8 minutes (longer if not using a gas hob) uncovered and without stirring until almost blackened.

Reduce the heat to medium, then drizzle in some olive oil and add the garlic and onion. Stir well and cook for a couple of minutes. Add the other vegetables along with about 2–3 tablespoons of water, and stir. Cover the pan with a lid and cook for 5 minutes.

Remove the lid and stir, then mix in the harissa and curry powder. Season with a generous amount of salt and pepper and stir. Add the coconut cream and stir until dissolved into the vegetable mixture and evenly combined. Cook for another 6–8 minutes, uncovered, until the vegetables are cooked to your liking, then squeeze in the lime juice, stir and serve.

GOES WELL WITH

Three Ways with Rice *(see pages 20–3)* *or Traybaked Ludicrously Good Latke* *(see page 171).*

Green Beans with Tomato & Garlic

This is very much a classic dish in many cultures from the East, with different versions being popular in both Turkish and Arab cuisine. The key principle is vegetables cooked in plenty of olive oil, often with the addition of garlic and tomatoes, and I love it so much. Here's a simple version to make at home, that makes a great accompaniment to grilled halloumi, meats or fish.

SERVES 3–4

olive oil
5 fat garlic cloves, thinly sliced
200g (7oz) trimmed extra-fine green beans, halved
½ teaspoon ground cumin
¼ teaspoon ground cinnamon
400g (14oz) can chopped tomatoes
½ teaspoon caster sugar
Maldon sea salt flakes and freshly ground black pepper

Place a saucepan over a medium heat, pour in enough olive oil to generously coat the base and fry the garlic until the edges begin to turn golden.

Add the green beans, spices and a generous amount of salt and pepper and cook for 5 minutes, stirring occasionally. Then add the canned tomatoes and sugar, stir and cook, uncovered, for 10 minutes, stirring occasionally.

Cover the pan with a lid, leaving it slightly ajar, and cook for another 10 minutes, stirring occasionally. Remove the lid and continue cooking for about 10–15 minutes until the sauce reduces and thickens, and the green beans have softened. Check and adjust the seasoning if desired, then serve.

GOES WELL WITH

My Family Traybake (see page 145) or Afghani Qorma Kofta (see page 186).

Sesame, Garlic & Tahini Spinach

This is one of my favourite ways to enjoy spinach. I love garlic with spinach, but the toasted sesame seeds, tahini and lemon here really take it to the next level, so much so that you might not want to share, hence serving 1–2 people. When, on the other hand, you're feeling generous, the recipe is easily doubled.

SERVES 1–2

1 tablespoon sesame seeds
olive oil
3 fat garlic cloves, thinly sliced
250g (9oz) baby spinach leaves
1 heaped tablespoon tahini
good squeeze of lemon juice
Maldon sea salt flakes and freshly ground black pepper

Heat a small dry frying pan over a medium-high heat, add the sesame seeds and toast for a few minutes, stirring occasionally to ensure they brown evenly. Remove from the pan and set aside.

Return the pan to the heat and drizzle in some olive oil. Once hot, add the garlic and cook until golden around the edges. Add the spinach leaves and stir quickly to prevent the garlic from burning and cook until wilted. Increase the heat and cook until any liquid the spinach has released has evaporated, but don't let it burn. Add the tahini and mix in along with some salt and pepper.

Squeeze in the lemon juice and mix again until the tahini is evenly blended. Serve sprinkled with the toasted sesame seeds, and enjoy.

GOES WELL WITH

Chicken & Potato Traybake with Za'atar & Lemon (see page 148) or Sticky Roasted Salmon with Tamarind & Chilli (see page 190).

Okra with Tomato & Garlic

Okra is by far one of the most misunderstood vegetables in existence. But if you know what to do with it, it is absolutely delicious. From stews to okra fries and so much more, I really love it. This treatment is popular in many different countries in the East, sometimes called *bamia bil zeit* in Arabic or *bamya zeytinyağlı* (zey-tin-yah-luh) if you're Turkish. *Bil zeit* and *zeytinyağlı* mean 'in oil', where a range of vegetables are cooked simply with good olive oil and usually tomato as a base. The trick with cooking okra, to avoid any off-putting sliminess, is the less you stir it, the better – just lightly shake the pan occasionally instead.

SERVES 4–6

olive oil
6–8 fat garlic cloves, thinly sliced
2 tablespoons tomato purée
1 teaspoon ground cumin
½ teaspoon ground cinnamon
350g (12oz) okra (the smaller, the better)
400g (14oz) can chopped tomatoes
1 teaspoon caster sugar
Maldon sea salt flakes and freshly ground black pepper

Place a saucepan over a medium-high heat, pour in enough olive oil to generously coat the base and fry the garlic for a few minutes until the edges begin to turn golden. Stir in the tomato purée and spices and cook them for a few minutes.

Add the okra and quickly and carefully coat the okra with the flavourings. Reduce the heat to medium, then add the canned tomatoes, sugar and a generous amount of salt and pepper and stir well – the best time to stir the ingredients is now while the okra is still raw. Cover the pan with a lid and cook for 20–25 minutes, shaking the pan a couple of times during cooking to avoid burning.

Remove the lid and check that the okra is cooked (I like mine to have a little bite), then check and adjust the seasoning, adding more salt and pepper if needed, before serving.

GOES WELL WITH

Firecracker Cauliflower Pilaf Traybake (see page 157) or Afghani Qorma Kofta (see page 186).

Sweet Pickled Broccoli & Cauliflower Stir-fry

I absolutely love broccoli and cauliflower and I'm always looking for new ways to eat it because the whole family also adore them both. This is sweet, a little spicy, tangy and delicious, and makes eating broccoli and cauliflower a real joy.

SERVES 3–4

olive oil
1 teaspoon cumin seeds
1 teaspoon black mustard seeds
250-300g (9–10½oz) broccoli florets, halved or quartered if large
250-300g (9–10½oz) cauliflower florets, sliced 1cm (½ inch) thick
½ teaspoon ground cinnamon
½ teaspoon chilli flakes
1 teaspoon ground turmeric
1 teaspoon garlic granules
1 tablespoon ginger purée/paste, or a thumb-sized piece of fresh ginger, finely grated
2 tablespoons white wine vinegar
1 tablespoon caster sugar
1–2 tablespoons water, if needed
Maldon sea salt and freshly ground black pepper

Put a drizzle of olive oil in a large frying pan over a medium-high heat. Add the cumin seeds and mustard seeds. Once the seeds start to pop, add the broccoli and cauliflower and stir quickly to coat them in the seeds.

Add the cinnamon, chilli flakes, turmeric, garlic granules and ginger to the pan, followed by the wine vinegar and sugar, then season with salt and pepper and stir quickly to combine. If the spices stick to the pan, add a tablespoon or so of water as needed and stir quickly. Cook for 3–4 minutes until the broccoli and cauliflower are just cooked but still retain some crunch, then serve immediately.

GOES WELL WITH

Sticky Honey, Lime & Harissa Sausage Meatballs (see page 91), Sweet & Spicy Spatchcocked Chicken (see page 176) or Sticky Roasted Salmon with Tamarind & Chilli (see page 190).

Sweet Treats

Need a dessert or sugary delight? Look no further... From morning pastries, perfect pairings with tea or coffee or showstopping desserts that are oh-so-simple but oh-so-impressive – no skill is required to make my easy desserts. However, be warned, these recipes are very addictive and you may find yourself visiting this chapter more than you should...

VEGETARIAN

Strawberry Tea-ramisu

Ok... I have to hold my hands up here and say that this is not actually a version of a tiramisu because I'm not using mascarpone, coffee or eggs! However, it is a very easy method and, if I do say so myself, a rather delightful dessert which doesn't even need much refrigeration time, so a winner for me on many levels. Top with anything you like – I sometimes use nuts, chocolate shavings and even sprinkles (I always have an assortment of sprinkles in the house!). Make it as fun and colourful or as elegant and sophisticated as you like.

SERVES 6–9

300ml (10fl oz) boiling water
2 Earl Grey teabags
1 heaped tablespoon caster sugar
600ml (20fl oz) double cream
finely grated zest of 2 unwaxed limes and juice of ½
seeds from 3 green cardamom pods, ground using a pestle and mortar
1 teaspoon vanilla bean paste
6 tablespoons icing sugar
32 sponge fingers
400g (14oz) strawberries, hulled and cut into 5mm (¼ inch) thick slices

You will need a 20cm (8 inch) square dish (preferably glass so you can see the pretty layers).

Pour the boiling water into a measuring jug, pop in your teabags and set a timer for exactly 4 minutes. Once infused, stir well and then squeeze out and discard the bags. Sweeten the tea with the caster sugar and leave to cool.

Meanwhile, pour the cream into a mixing bowl and add the zest of 1½ limes (reserving the rest for topping the dessert) and the lime juice, the cardamom, vanilla and icing sugar. Using an electric hand whisk, whip until stiff peaks start to form but the mixture remains pillowy soft and spoonable. Set aside.

Take 2 sponge fingers at a time and dunk them 4 times in the tea, shake off any excess, then use to tightly line the base of your dish – you will need 2 lines of 8 sponge fingers.

Arrange the strawberry slices, slightly overlapping, to cover the sponge fingers. Add half the cream mixture and smooth over. Repeat the soaking and layering of the remaining sponge fingers, cover with strawberry slices, then finish with the remaining cream mixture. Top with any leftover strawberry slices and grate over the remaining zest of ½ lime. Chill in the refrigerator for a minimum of an hour (up to overnight) before decorating and serving.

PALLARÈS
SOLSONA

VEGETARIAN

Vanilla Cheesecake with Lime, Black Pepper, Cherries & Berries

I do love a cheesecake, but I'm difficult to please and I usually prefer a plain cheesecake with just a little added fruit. Making a good cheesecake doesn't need to be complicated and this little number is a classic vanilla flavour, but the fresh fruit topping really adds to it and turns it into a celebratory dessert.

SERVES 8–10

250g (9oz) digestive biscuits
100g (3½oz) unsalted butter, melted
200g (7oz) mascarpone cheese
200g (7oz) full-fat cream cheese
2 heaped teaspoons best-quality vanilla bean paste
150g (5½oz) icing sugar
600ml (20fl oz) double cream

For the topping
250g (9oz) strawberries, hulled and quartered
200g (7oz) cherries, pitted and halved
200g (7oz) blueberries, halved
3 tablespoons caster sugar
finely grated zest of 1 unwaxed lime
½ teaspoon coarsely ground black pepper

Line a 22cm (8½ inch) round springform cake tin with a square of baking paper and lock it into the base so that the edges of the paper remain outside the tin.

Crush the biscuits in a food bag with a rolling pin or in a bowl with the end of a rolling pin. Decant the biscuit crumbs into a bowl (if not already in a bowl), pour over the melted butter and stir together. Add the biscuit mixture to the lined tin and press down firmly to make an even base, then refrigerate for 30 minutes.

Mix the mascarpone, cream cheese and vanilla together in a bowl really well until evenly combined and set aside.

Sift the icing sugar into a mixing bowl, then add the cream. Use an electric hand whisk to whip the cream and sugar until the mixture forms stiff peaks. Gradually and gently fold in the cheese mixture a little at a time until it is all incorporated, then pour over the biscuit base, smooth over and chill in the refrigerator for at least 2–3 hours or overnight.

Mix all the topping ingredients together in a bowl and leave to sit for 20 minutes (don't make this too far in advance or the fruit juices will leak). Stir again and spoon over the cheesecake before serving. Serve any leftover berries on the side.

VEGETARIAN

Salted Peanut Baklava Roll-ups

I love baklava, but it hasn't escaped my notice how expensive nuts have become, so I turned to peanuts, not only for economy but also because I rather like the salty flavour in a baklava. I've also broken from tradition and ditched the syrup in this instance in favour of icing sugar. It makes for a slightly different treat, but doesn't scrimp on satisfaction one little bit.

MAKES 14

200g (7oz) salted peanuts

2 tablespoons caster sugar

7 sheets (or 270g/9½oz packet) of filo pastry (each about 480 x 250mm/19 x 10 inches)

100g (3½oz) unsalted butter, melted

icing sugar, to serve

Preheat the oven to 200°C, 180°C fan (400°F), Gas Mark 6. Line a baking tray with baking paper.

Blitz the peanuts in a mini food processor until ground as finely as possible. Decant into a bowl, add the caster sugar and mix together well until evenly combined.

Unroll your filo pastry sheets on a clean chopping board and stack them neatly on top of each other. Cut all the sheets in half lengthways to make 14 long pieces.

Have the melted butter and a pastry brush to hand.

Divide the peanut mixture into 14 equal portions by weighing them out for accuracy.

Sprinkle one portion of nuts evenly in a line down the middle of a piece of pastry, leaving a 5cm (2 inch) border.

Fold over 5cm (2 inches) of the pastry ends. Next, fold one of the long pastry edges over the nuts and brush the top of it with melted butter. Fold the remaining long pastry edge over the buttered pastry to seal.

Starting at one end, roll up the pastry as tightly as you can until you reach the last 3cm (1 inch), then quickly dab on a little melted butter and continue rolling it up to seal. Place on the lined tray. Repeat with the remaining peanut mixture and pastry pieces.

Brush melted butter all over the top and sides of the baklava rolls, then bake for 22–25 minutes until golden brown. Remove from the oven and leave to cool completely, then dust with as much icing sugar as you like and serve.

Passion Fruit, Lime & Coconut Cake

Cake is one of my all-time favourite foods and I love to combine this with exotic fruits, especially when it's cold and miserable here at home and I want a nice slice of something tropical. All my cake recipes are ridiculously easy to throw together, because life is too short to spend hours making things that get demolished in minutes. This is a very moist, almost creamy-textured cake, and I love nothing more than a slice of this with a cup of strong Yorkshire tea.

SERVES 8

- **3 eggs**
- **200g (7oz) caster sugar**
- **240ml (8½fl oz) carton coconut cream**
- **1 teaspoon vanilla bean extract**
- **6 tablespoons olive oil**
- **finely grated zest of 2 unwaxed limes and juice of 1**
- **4 passion fruits, halved and pulp and seeds scooped out with a spoon, 2 reserved for the topping**
- **150g (5½oz) plain flour**
- **100g (3½oz) ground almonds**
- **25g (1oz) desiccated coconut, plus an extra 1 heaped tablespoon for decorating**
- **1 teaspoon baking powder**
- **3 tablespoons apricot jam**

Preheat the oven to 180°C, 160°C fan (350°F), Gas Mark 4. Line a 20cm (8 inch) round springform cake tin with baking paper (or you can use a 22cm/8½ inch cast-iron pot).

Beat the eggs, sugar, coconut cream and vanilla together in a mixing bowl until evenly combined. Add the olive oil, lime zest and juice and the pulp and seeds of the 2 passion fruits and mix again. Add the flour, ground almonds, desiccated coconut and baking powder and mix well until the batter is smooth.

Pour the batter into the lined tin and bake for 1 hour until a skewer or knife inserted into the centre of the cake comes out clean. Remove from the oven and leave to cool completely in the tin.

Mix the reserved passion fruit pulp and seeds with the apricot jam in a small bowl. Spread over the top of the cooled cake, sprinkle with the extra desiccated coconut and serve.

VEGETARIAN

Spiced Sugar Palmiers

I've loved these crispy little sugar-crusted gems since I was a kid. Having realized how easy they are to make, I have stopped spending lots of money buying them from bakeries and now make my own instead. These are my very easy (and slightly rougher-looking) version of the classic, and are all too easy to eat in large quantities.

MAKES ABOUT 22

- **1 x 320g (11¼oz) ready-rolled all-butter puff pastry sheet (about 350 x 230mm/14 x 9 inches)**
- **50g (1¾oz) caster sugar, plus an extra 60g (2¼oz)**
- **1 teaspoon ground cinnamon**
- **½ teaspoon ground ginger**
- **seeds from 3 fat green cardamom pods, ground using a pestle and mortar**
- **25g (1oz) unsalted butter, melted**
- **1 egg, beaten**

Preheat the oven to 200°C, 180°C fan (400°F), Gas Mark 6. Line a large baking tray with baking paper.

Unroll your pastry sheet and peel it off the paper it comes rolled up in. Sprinkle the 50g (1¾oz) caster sugar evenly over the paper, then press the pastry sheet back on to the sugared paper so that the sugar sticks to the pastry.

Put the remaining 60g (2¼oz) caster sugar in a bowl with the spices and mix together.

Brush the bare side of the pastry sheet all over with the melted butter, then sprinkle with the spiced sugar.

Take one long side of pastry and roll it up very tightly, stopping in the centre. Roll up the other side to meet it in the middle. Carefully cut the roll into about 22 slices, each 1cm (½ inch) thick. I should point out here, in case you think you're doing something wrong, that the slices will naturally uncurl and you will lose some sugar, so once you've cut each slice, gently press down and flatten them lightly before transferring them to your lined tray. And don't worry, we won't be wasting any sugar left behind, either.

Once all the palmiers are on the tray with a little space around each, brush them with the beaten egg to glaze, then collect the stray sugar and sprinkle it over the tops. Bake for 20 minutes until golden brown. Remove from the oven and leave to cool before enjoying.

Date, Pecan & Tamarind Drizzle Cake

This is a fantastic little loaf cake inspired by the familiar flavours of the East. Studded with dates and pecans, warmed by a little cinnamon and finished with a tamarind drizzle, it may just become your best afternoon treat.

SERVE 8

3 eggs
150g (5½oz) caster sugar
1 teaspoon vanilla bean paste
1 teaspoon ground cinnamon
150g (5½oz) salted or unsalted butter, melted and cooled
150g (5½oz) plain flour
1 teaspoon baking powder
2 tablespoons milk
100g (3½oz) dates, pitted, halved and roughly chopped or cut into thin strips
100g (3½oz) pecan nuts, roughly chopped

For the icing
100g (3½oz) icing sugar, plus extra if needed
2 tablespoons tamarind paste (some brands contain salt and some don't – you can use either)

Preheat the oven to 180°C, 160°C fan (350°F), Gas Mark 4. Line a 900g (2lb) loaf tin with baking paper.

Beat the eggs, caster sugar, vanilla and cinnamon together in a mixing bowl until well combined. Add the melted butter, flour and baking powder and mix together, then add the milk, dates and half the pecans and mix until just combined.

Pour the batter into the lined tin and bake for 1 hour or until a skewer or knife inserted into the centre comes out clean. Remove from the oven and leave the cake to cool for a few minutes, then turn it out on to a wire rack and leave to cool completely.

While the cake is cooling, make the icing by mixing the icing sugar and tamarind paste together in a bowl. You may find you need more icing sugar, depending on the type of tamarind paste you are using, but just ensure your icing has a thick, just-pourable consistency that will stick to your cake.

Once the cake is cool, top with the icing, decorate with reserved pecans and leave to set before serving.

VEGETARIAN

Dark Chocolate, Almond & Ras el Hanout Torte

This is one of those perfect desserts that is not only incredibly delicious, but it's feather light and gluten-free so perfect for everyone. I like to finish it with icing sugar on top, but you could use cocoa powder if you prefer.

SERVES 6 – 8

5 eggs, separated
100g (3½oz) caster sugar
200g (7oz) best-quality dark chocolate, broken up
175ml (6fl oz) light olive oil
100g (3½oz) ground almonds
1 teaspoon vanilla bean paste
1 teaspoon ground cinnamon
2 teaspoons ras el hanout
15g (½oz) flaked almonds (optional)
1 heaped tablespoon icing sugar

Preheat the oven to 200°C, 180°C fan (400°F), Gas Mark 6. Line a 20cm (8 inch) diameter springform cake tin with baking paper.

Put the egg yolks in a large mixing bowl with the sugar and whisk until pale and fluffy.

Melt the chocolate in a heatproof bowl set over a pan of gently simmering water, then once melted, stir in the olive oil until the mixture is smooth and fully combined. Leave to cool for 10 minutes, then add the ground almonds, vanilla, cinnamon and ras el hanout and mix well. Stir the chocolate mixture into the bowl with the egg yolks.

In a separate bowl, whisk the egg whites using an electric hand whisk until they reach the stiff-peak stage. Gently fold them, a little at a time – in about 5 spoonfuls – into the chocolate mixture until combined.

Pour the cake mixture into the prepared tin, scatter flaked almonds over the top if using, then bake for 20 minutes.

Remove from the oven and allow to cool completely in the tin on a wire rack before serving. The cake may collapse slightly on cooling, but this is perfectly normal. Dust icing sugar over the top before serving.

Orange & Pistachio Cream Cheese Danishes

When I was a kid, my grandma would buy whole trays of Danish pastries and bring them home as a treat. This memory has stuck with me, and my love for Danish pastries of every description knows no bounds. These are easy, impressive and absolutely delicious! Try them and see.

MAKES 6

75g (2¾oz) pistachio nuts or slivers

1 egg, beaten

100g (3½oz) full-fat cream cheese

2 tablespoons caster sugar

finely grated zest of 1 unwaxed orange, plus the whole orange

1 x 320g (11¼oz) ready-rolled puff pastry sheet (about 350 x 230mm/14 x 9 inches)

For the drizzle

3 tablespoons icing sugar

1½ teaspoons milk

Preheat the oven to 220°C, 200°C fan (425°F), Gas Mark 7. Line a large baking tray with baking paper.

Blitz the pistachios in a mini food processor until they are ground as finely as possible.

Mix together half the beaten egg, the cream cheese, sugar, orange zest and 50g (1¾oz) of the ground pistachios in a bowl.

Cut the pastry sheet into 6 equal squarish pieces. Divide the cream cheese mixture into 6 portions and spoon one portion in the centre of each pastry piece – do not spread it out.

Using a sharp knife, cut a disc of peel off the top and base of each orange, then working from the top of the fruit downwards, cut away the rest of the remaining peel and pith in strips, just enough to expose the orange flesh, until the entire orange is peeled. Cut the oranges in half from top to bottom, then slice each half across the middle into 6 pieces. Place 2 orange slices slightly overlapping on top of the cream cheese mixture on each pastry piece.

Pinch together two corners on each side of the pastry square to make a boat shape with the filing in the centre – some exposed pastry should be visible inside. Place the pastries spaced apart on the lined tray, then use a pastry brush to brush all the exposed pastry all over with the remaining beaten egg. Bake for 20 minutes or until golden brown. Remove from the oven and leave to cool completely.

Mix the icing sugar and milk together, then use a teaspoon to drizzle it all over the pastries and finish with a sprinkling of the remaining ground pistachios.

Spiced Orange & Apricot Croissant Bread Pudding

This really is a unique and absolutely delicious version of a bread pudding made using croissants, which have butter built-in for an extra-luxurious result without any extra effort!

SERVES 6–8

8 day-old all-butter croissants, sliced into 2cm (¾ inch) thick pieces
100g (3½oz) dried apricots, each cut into 3 strips
generous handful of flaked almonds
25g (1oz) caster sugar
icing sugar, to serve (optional)

For the custard
3 eggs
300ml (10fl oz) double cream, plus extra to serve
350ml (12fl oz) milk
2 teaspoons vanilla extract
finely grated zest of 2 unwaxed oranges and juice of 1
1 teaspoon ground turmeric
1 teaspoon ground cinnamon
1 teaspoon ground ginger
150g (5½oz) caster sugar
50g (1¾oz) unsalted butter, melted

Using a hand whisk, whisk all the custard ingredients together in a mixing bowl until evenly combined.

Select a large rectangular ovenproof dish and lay all the croissant slices in the dish, slightly overlapping each other and really packing them all in. Then stuff the apricot strips into the crevices between the croissant pieces and around the edges and corners. Ladle the custard mixture over the croissants until every bit is covered and then leave to absorb for 15 minutes.

Meanwhile, preheat the oven to 200°C, 180°C fan (400°F), Gas Mark 6.

Sprinkle the flaked almonds and caster sugar evenly over the pudding and bake for 25–35 minutes or so until the top has browned and the custard has set and is no longer liquid. Remove from the oven and serve with a dusting of icing sugar, if you wish, but, in my opinion, a drizzle of double cream makes it extra indulgent!

Index

D

E

F

G

UK–US Glossary

aubergine .... eggplant
baking paper .... parchment paper
baking tray .... baking sheet
bicarbonate of soda .... baking soda
butter beans .... lima beans
caster sugar .... superfine sugar
chestnut mushrooms .... brown or cremini mushrooms
chicken mince .... ground chicken
chicory .... endive
chilli flakes .... red pepper flakes
coriander .... cilantro
clingfilm .... plastic wrap
cornflour .... cornstarch
courgette .... zucchini
crème fraîche .... can be substituted with sour cream
dark chocolate .... bittersweet chocolate
desiccated coconut .... shredded unsweetened coconut
double cream .... heavy cream
filo pastry .... phyllo dough
flaked almonds .... slivered almonds
frying pan .... skillet
hob .... stove
icing .... frosting
icing sugar .... confectioners' sugar
jam .... jelly
kitchen paper .... paper towels
Maldon sea salt flakes .... kosher salt
muslin .... cheesecloth
natural yogurt .... plain yogurt
nigella seeds .... black onion seeds/kalonji
passata .... strained tomatoes
pepper .... bell pepper
plain flour .... all-purpose flour
prawns .... shrimp
pul biber chilli flakes .... Aleppo pepper
self-raising flour .... self-rising flour
sieve .... strainer
sponge fingers .... ladyfingers
spring onions .... scallions
stock cube .... bouillon cube
sweetcorn cobs .... ears of corn
tea towel .... kitchen/dish towel
Tenderstem broccoli .... broccolini
tomato purée .... tomato paste
tin .... pan

Acknowledgements

Thank you to Octopus Publishing Group, for always supporting my ideas and producing such beautiful books. A special mention to my publisher Kate Fox for being so supportive and brilliant since she joined the team – thanks for handling the madness so beautifully!

To Sybella Stephens, we will miss you immensely, but thank you for all your hard work on an incredible 9 books.

Enormous thanks to Jaz Bahra and Jonathan Christie for always creating stunning books with a unique design every time.

Thank you to Chloë, Lucy, Ailie, Matt, Kieron & Matilda for all their hard work with publicity and marketing.

Thanks to Lucy and the sales team for all their behind-the-scenes hard work in getting the books to where they need to be.

Thank you also to Charlie King for your hands-on enthusiasm with my books and ongoing support with my work.

A huge thank to you to my dear friend and photographer Kris Kirkham, who I couldn't imagine working without. Your work has enabled me to illustrate recipes that jump off the page. Thank you to your brilliant assistants Rob and Pheobe, too.

Thank you to the ever-patient Laura Field, my food stylist, for always making my recipes look so beautiful, and for understanding how important it is for me to keep things real and simple. You, Lizzie and Hilary are just brilliant, and I really appreciate your patience with my work and me!

To Agathe, you bring the food to life with stunning props and colours, and your laugh fills the room like nobody else's ever will.

Thank you, as always, to Richard and Trish Sinclair for the most wonderful venue and shoot studio that now feels like a home. Thanks to Alfie for putting up with us working around you and not being able to stop and play all the time.

To my brilliant agent Martine Carter; I feel like your patience gets tested more and more over the years with my madcap ideas and 1001 questions... thanks for all your patience and reassurance – there is a sainthood waiting for you in the years to come! I very much appreciate the support and friendship over the last 14 years – you are family to us.

And finally, a big, huge thank you to my family... my Mama (and PA) who has to taste everything, give opinions (even at the risk of me barking back when tired), and who supports everything I do. You're the Thelma to my Louise and I couldn't do it without you.

To my wonderful husband Stephen, I've said it before and I'll say it again... this is all for us... all of it – thank you for supporting me, championing me and always reassuring me that I'm sane when sometimes it all feels a bit mad and overwhelming. Love, love, love you always.